DAVID BECKHAM
THE GREAT BETRAYAL

DAVID BECKHAM
THE GREAT BETRAYAL

VIRGINIA BLACKBURN

JOHN BLAKE

Published by
John Blake Publishing Ltd,
3 Bramber Court,2 Bramber Road,
London W14 9PB, England

First published in 2003

ISBN 1 84454 016 2

British Library Cataloguing-in-Publication Data: A catalogue record for this book is available from the British Library.

Design by ENVY

Printed and bound in Great Britain by Bookmarque

1 3 5 7 9 10 8 6 4 2

Papers used by John Blake Publishing Ltd are natural, recyclable products made from wood grown in sustainable forests. The manufacturing processes conform to the environmental regulations of the country of origin.

Contents

Chapter One

Los Angeles 2003

David and Victoria Beckham were ecstatic. It was mid-summer and the two of them, along with their sons Brooklyn and Romeo, were on a working holiday in the United States, designed to increase their already stratospheric profile still further and launch them in the one country in which they were still relatively unknown. So far it had gone beautifully: they had been feted in New York, appeared on nationwide television and had no reason to suspect that the summer would be anything other than a triumph.

The last leg of the tour was Los Angeles, where the duo were to present an MTV award – together, naturally – have screen tests and get some much-needed rest and relaxation. And so the family rented an £18,000-a-week luxury villa, complete with swimming pool, nestling in the heart of Beverly Hills. And it was here that David was resting on Tuesday, 10 June when he got a call from Tony Stephens, his agent. Tony asked if David had seen the official Manchester United website. No, replied David, he hadn't. In that case, said Tony, he should take a look – and fast.

Manchester United have released the following statement regarding David Beckham and Barcelona:

'Manchester United confirms that club officials have met Joan Laporta, the leading candidate for the presidency of Barcelona.

These meetings have resulted in an offer being made for the transfer of David Beckham to Barcelona.

'This offer is subject to a number of conditions and critically to Mr Laporta being elected president on Sunday 15 June and Barcelona subsequently reaching agreement with David Beckham on his personal cantract.

'Manchester United confirms that in the event that all of the conditions are fulfilled then the offer would be acceptable.'

David logged on and went to the website – and what he saw there almost made his heart stop beating. For there, utterly unbeknown to him, was an announcement:

David was absolutely shattered. It had been clear for some months now that he could no longer continue with Manchester United: relations between him and Sir Alex Ferguson, the man he had once regarded as a second father, were now so bad that the pair had not actually spoken for months. But this – David saw it as an absolute betrayal. For not only had there been an informal agreement between all the parties involved not to come to any decision until after the 15th – when the elections for the Barcelona presidency would take place – but no one had even bothered to tell him that the announcement had been made. It was the end of a beautiful relationship – between David and one of the most famous clubs in the world.

David lost no time in making his feelings known. 'David is devastated,' said a friend. 'He's been stabbed in the back and sold like a slave by Fergie and Man United while he's not even in Europe. This is United's first gambit to begin a bidding war for David. They want him out – and want as much cash as possible. And they're hoping that, by going public now, the phoney war is over and they can draw even bigger offers.'

That was almost certainly true. Real Madrid had been interested in David for some time now, but had

3

been offering only £15 million for the player, with the added possibility of swapping a few more players. United wanted – and eventually got – a great deal more and were all too aware that David had only another two years to run on his contract with them, after which he could leave for nothing.

But it was a shabby way to treat their greatest star and David authorised his management company, SFX, to speak on his behalf. 'David is very disappointed and surprised to learn of this statement and feels that he has been used as a political pawn in the Barcelona presidential elections,' said a spokesman. 'David's advisers have no plans to meet Mr Laporta or his representatives.'

David's father Ted was equally upset. Ted had been a lifelong supporter of United and it was he who had first installed in David an equal love of the club. 'I shall tell him not to go there,' he said. 'I don't want him to go just because a certain person wants him to go. It's a shame – his heart is with Manchester United. He is the hardest-working footballer I know. Like me, David is Man United through and through. It was all he ever wanted from life to play football for them and he still loves the club. I shall tell him not to go. I don't want him to go. He will not go. I want him to stay at United.' But it was too late. David's position was untenable.

And others in the industry spoke out. Footballer turned TV pundit Gary Lineker spoke for many when he agreed that David was being used. 'I think it's a bit of a farce until Laporta wins the election and that, from what I understand, is a long way off,' he said. 'It will be very hard for David but at least he has the right sort of people around him to advise him. But, from what I know, a deal is a long way off.'

The footballing legend George Best agreed. 'Beckham seems to be piggy in the middle and it is not fair when someone has given so much loyalty to one club when loyalty is so rare these days,' he said. 'He has certainly been loyal to Manchester United and I think he has been treated abysmally.'

Under the terms of his contract, David didn't actually have to leave but, had he chosen to stay, his life would have been a nightmare. He was no longer wanted at Old Trafford – by a certain person, at least – and, if he stayed, he could almost certainly have looked forward to a season sitting on the bench. He knew it, too, and on that same Tuesday gave an indication that he was ready to go. 'I am a Manchester United player ... as long as they want me, I'll stay,' he told the *Los Angeles Times*, then added, 'I have never said that I'd never move away from Manchester and I've never said that I'd end my career there.'

And so a train of events had been set in motion from which there was no backing out. It was a difficult time for David to have been caught in these talks: after the States, he and Victoria were planning to move on to the Far East, where Beckham was regarded as an idol. But the mess had to be sorted out – and fast. David did not want to go to Barcelona, he had made that perfectly clear – but another Spanish team wanted him and it was the obvious move for him to make.

A meeting was hastily arranged in Sardinia between Manchester United chief executive Peter Kenyon, with managing director David Gill, and Real fixers Pedro Lopez and José Angel Sanchez. A deal was hammered out, this time with David's knowledge and approval, and terms and conditions set. Meanwhile, David and Victoria flew back to Britain for a brief stay and it was there, while having a barbecue in the back garden of Beckingham Palace with Victoria's parents, that David finally decided to go.

And so, on 17 June, just less than a week after the row blew up, it was announced that David Beckham, the most famous member of Manchester United's 'Class of '92', was moving to Real Madrid in a deal worth £25 million to United and £30 million to David himself. It was for four years and he would be earning £120,000 a week. Everyone then rushed out to make statements about how much they all owed each other.

'I would like to publicly thank Sir Alex Ferguson for making me the player I am today,' said David in a display of graciousness that not everyone felt Fergie deserved. 'I will always hold precious memories of my time at Manchester United and Old Trafford as well as the players, who I regard as part of my family, and the brilliant fans who have given me so much support over the years and continue to do so.

'I recognise that this is an amazing opportunity for me at this stage in my career and a unique and exciting experience for my family. I know that I will always regret it later in life if I had turned down the chance to play at another great club like Real Madrid, which also has world-class players. I would like to thank other clubs who were interested in signing me, including Barcelona, and I wish them every success in the future, but I really want to play in the Champions League.

'I wish Manchester United the best of luck and, led by such an inspirational captain as Roy Keane, I am sure they will continue to go from strength to strength.'

It was an exceptionally generous message to all concerned and one that was totally in keeping with David's character. Apart from the occasional touches of bad temper on the field, David is a remarkable man and a remarkable footballer. United had lost a rare prize.

Given that he had, as ever, got exactly what he wanted, Ferguson could also afford to be cordial. 'I've known David since he was 11 years of age, and it's been a pleasure to see him grow and develop into the player he has become,' he said politely. 'David has been an integral part of all the successes that Manchester United have achieved in the last decade. I would like to wish him and his family every success in the future and thank him for his service to the club.'

David's management company, SFX, also poured oil on the swirling waters. 'Manchester United have been professional, fair and open in all of their dealings with David – he will always have the greatest memories of his time at Old Trafford,' said a spokesman.

And Peter Kenyon also said his bit. 'While we are sad to see David go after so many years at Old Trafford, we believe this is a good deal for the club, and we now look forward to building on the success of last season's championship title,' he said. 'We wish David all the best in his new career in Spain and thank him for his fantastic contribution to the team's achievements in the last decade. We have worked closely with David's advisers throughout the past few weeks and thank them for their co-operation.'

It was, quite literally, the end of an era. David had been part of the 'Class of '92', a group of young players picked in the early 1990s and nurtured under the then youth coach Eric Harrison. It also included such players as Ryan Giggs, Paul Scholes, Nicky Butt and the brothers Gary and Phil Neville, and right from the start showed exceptional promise, winning the FA Youth Cup. The six went on to become senior internationals, starting 1,795 games for the club. They also played leading roles in six league title campaigns, the Champions League success of 1999 and two FA Cup wins – exceptional progress by anyone's standards. And now David was the first of the six to go. Under the terms of the deal, £5.2 million would be paid on completion of the sale, with £12.24 million being paid over the next four years. A further £7 million was to be paid if Real did well in the Champions League.

There was widespread disgust at the way David had been treated, though, and a sense that, for once, Sir Alex had let his heart rule his head. It seemed his exasperation with David's lifestyle had finally got the better of him, leading him to rid United of its greatest asset. 'I get a bit sick when I hear Ferguson's comments about wishing him well and all that – it's a load of rubbish,' said former Manchester United manager Tommy Docherty. 'He should have kept the boy at Old Trafford. He did nothing wrong. He was a credit to the club and his country, both on and off pitch. David was left with no alternative, he was forced out of Old Trafford – there's no other word for it.

'I mean, if you look, the alternatives that the boy had was maybe play in the reserves for two years or sit and wait for a Bosman free transfer. That's not David's nature – David just wants to play.' But he had no doubt that David would do well. 'When you leave Man United, there's only one other club you can go to and that's Real Madrid. David's a great player and a great captain and going to Madrid – he's only going to become a better player and the people who are going to benefit from that is England.'

The two families concerned, the Beckhams and

Victoria's parents, the Adamses, reacted very differently to the news. Ted Beckham had already made it clear that he didn't want David to go and, so, unsurprisingly, he was unable to hide his disappointment. 'I'm not really very happy,' he said. 'As you know, I am a big fan of Manchester United and I'm not pleased he's going. I'm a bit fed up, as you can probably tell from my voice. It is an unfortunate turn of events. I have been asked not to say anything about it, although there is plenty I want to say. But I dare not say what I really think. I'd rather not say anything. I feel choked that he's going and the way he's had to go.'

Tony Adams, Victoria's father, took completely the opposite point of view. David was extremely close to Victoria's whole family, and it was telling that it was while talking to her parents rather than his own mother or father – they are separated – that he came to his decision. Tony revealed his feelings during a debate on LBC Radio in London, when he rang in to offer his point of view. Asked how he felt about the move, he replied, 'Fine. It's early days but both of them have got their families behind them. We'll obviously be doing lots of trips. It's great that the children will be living in an environment where they'll be able to learn another language. I think everyone's going to benefit. It makes such a change to hear – particularly the journalists – saying nice things about them.'

Asked if it was always going to be Real Madrid, Tony replied, 'If you look at the facts then yes, I guess it was. The fact that they're in the Champions League and all the players they have. They're the sort of people that David does tend to idolise, so when you look at it from an obvious point of view, then, yes, I guess it was.'

Tony went on to admit that, yes, Victoria would have preferred Milan and that David would miss Manchester. 'David is very good friends with most of the players but, then again, life goes on and he'll keep in touch with them.' He also revealed that Brooklyn had inherited his father's talent. 'He shows a hell of a lot of ability, although Victoria's always said she'd rather he became a tennis player or a lawyer, but from an early age he's always kicked a ball straight.' Tony was then asked about his daughter's relationship with Ferguson. 'Can I use the famous "no comment"?' he replied.

Real itself was over the moon. 'We are delighted with David's arrival, a strategic signing who will contribute to making us a more competitive club and team,' said sports director Jorge Valdano. 'It has been David's firm and unflinching will to play for Madrid which made this possible. He's a great professional.'

He went on to make it clear both that Real did not poach David and that David's lifestyle was not a problem to the club. 'We didn't take Beckham out of Manchester United,' he said. 'They opened the door for him to leave. All we have done is receive him with open arms. Beckham is very passionate about football and very professional. You get the impression that football is the most important thing to him. I think the idea that Beckham cares too much about the showbusiness side of his life is wrong. He has the ability to concentrate on his football, despite all the media pressure on him because of his high profile. And I can assure you that Beckham's arrival will not prove a problem to our team spirit. He will not contaminate the dressing room because of his status.'

And Madrid's two daily sports newspapers were ecstatic. The previous day *Marca* had run a picture of him in Real's all-white shirt under the headline 'Beckham in 10 Days' and followed it up with 'Said And Done'. *Ace*, meanwhile, ran a headline saying, 'Sixth Heaven', which referred to Real's other five footballing superstars: Ronaldo, Figo, Zidane, Raul and Roberto Carlos. The crisis was over, the deal was done. David was going to Spain.

And when the Beckham entourage hit Madrid a few weeks later for David to take a much-publicised medical – indeed, it was filmed – it fulfilled all expectations. The city went wild. 'Beckham: The Madness Arrives', proclaimed *Marca* as David was driven to the Zarzuela clinic, having flown into town on a Gulfstream jet that landed at El Torrejon, a military base, because the main airport was considered too open. He then continued in a motorcade accompanied by six police outriders and a handful of paparazzi on motorbikes before taking that medical. 'He is in perfect physical condition to play football for Real Madrid,' said the club's head doctor, Alfonso del Corral, as teenage girls quite literally wept outside. It was about as anti-Ferguson a scene as you could imagine – and a clear indication as to why it had all gone so wrong.

It was, in fact, a crisis that had been brewing for years. Ever since he met Victoria in 1997 Beckham had made it quite clear that she, and later the couple's sons, was the most important element in his life. And, while Sir Alex Ferguson have could just about tolerated that, what he could not take was the growing publicity surrounding the two. Fergie is a traditional footballer whereas David isn't a traditional anything and his one-time mentor could not understand the make-up-wearing, party-going, home-loving celebrity that David had become.

Just a few months earlier, Sir Alex had made his feelings clear. 'He has a lifestyle he enjoys and I do not know how he does it,' he said. 'I don't know how he can lead that life because of the attention he gets all the time. Television has projected football players in to a superstar status, which is not really justified. David enjoys it. He realises he has a star status and a lot of it is by his own design. He has cultivated it himself. He likes to dress in a certain way, changes his hairstyle and is not aware how that is portrayed by a lot of people. I say that to him time and again.'

Fergie went on to praise David's talent and good manners, but the message was clear. The boss didn't like his star player's lifestyle and wanted him to tone it down. David, on the other hand, loved it and fully intended to keep going as he was.

Tellingly, after he left, United captain Roy Keane made it clear that he thought Ferguson was right and that United would not necessarily suffer. In his autobiography he had asked whether United teammates were 'more interested in their Rolex watches, garages full of cars and mansions' – a comment that was taken to be a clear dig at David. He was also becoming increasingly close to Sir Alex, which led some observers to wonder whether that dig might have influenced the United boss finally to take action. Keane was diplomatic but candid about the recent upset when asked if the deterioration in David and Ferguson's relationship had been the deciding factor.

'You would have to ask the player and the manager about that,' he said. 'All I know is that our manager will always do what he thinks is best for Manchester United and, if he thinks selling Becks is the best thing for Manchester United, then he will do it. It is unfortunate because he is a top player, but the manager has sold a lot of top players over the years and the club has gone on. It is what football is all about. It doesn't matter who the player is – players will always come and go. It is a business and, if a club gets a good price for the player, they will have to look at it. It is the same for me ... So you just get on with it and, while you miss him as a player, you have to be a little bit selfish and maybe just look after yourself and make sure that you are staying at a club like Manchester United because we are the biggest club in the world.' If he'd added, 'Yah, boo, sucks,' on after it, the message could not have been clearer.

The tensions between Beckham and Ferguson had been mounting for some years now, but it was in the 2001/2 season when they finally reached boiling point. David was due to sign a new contract, but all sorts of obstacles began to present themselves that had never been there before. United had become unhappy with David's many lucrative sponsorship deals and was thought to be trying to cut them back. David, meanwhile, began to feel that he was not being treated with the respect he deserved. He ended up with a pay packet of £95,000 a week, but the damage was done, especially as far as David was concerned. He had given a good deal of his life to Manchester United, had sworn over and over that he never wanted to leave but now, for the first time ever, he began to feel that his future really might lie elsewhere.

Speaking in a glitzy showbiz ceremony in Madrid at the beginning of July 2003, David revealed that he'd known the writing was on the wall for some time. 'Six or seven months ago, the rumours about my future began,' he said. 'From that point everything was fine, but I became totally clear that I had to leave two or three weeks ago. Now everything has turned out for the best. Real Madrid are one of the biggest clubs in the world and, while the decision to leave United was really hard, the decision to join Real was not.

'It is a dream come true. It is a big challenge, but one I'm looking forward to. I can't wait to start training and playing. Real sent me a shirt through the post. This is the first time I've worn it in public, but I have been wearing it round the house. Brooklyn has already got one because I always try to bring back a strip from the local team of anywhere I go in the world. Now he is looking forward to going out in it.'

Clearly trouble had been brewing for months, but matters finally came to a head in February 2003 when Sir Alex lost his temper in a way that was, even by his own standards, terrifying. United lost 2–0 at home to Arsenal in the FA Cup: Sir Alex stormed into the players' dressing room afterwards and savagely kicked a boot which went in David's direction. The boot hit David in the eye, requiring stitches.

David was absolutely, utterly livid. Matters had sunk to an all-time low – and this was the man, remember, who David had idolised as a teenager and respected as a man. It is one thing to have your manager criticise your lifestyle; it is quite another to have him kick boots in your face. There was never any question that it was a deliberate injury but, even so, matters had got completely out of hand.

Fergie tried to pass off the injury as a 'freakish incident'. 'If I tried it a hundred times or a million times it could not happen again – if it did, I would have carried on playing,' he said. 'Contrary to reports, David did not have two stitches in his head – he had no stitches. It was a graze that was dealt with by the doctor. There was no problem and we move on. That is all there is to be said for it.'

David, however, told a different story, not least by his appearance. He appeared the next day with a hairband holding his hair off his forehead so that everyone could see the damage that had been done. Meanwhile, a spokesman put his side to the public. 'David did not want stitches at first,' he said, 'but, two hours after the game, blood was still dripping from the wound and the club doctor visited David's house and fixed two steri-strips to stop the bleeding.'

Manchester United tried to play the incident down. 'Whatever happens in the dressing room remains private,' said a spokesman – except this time it didn't. David was parading his injuries in front of the cameras. No one was in any doubt what had happened back then. (Actually – that is not entirely true. There is an alternative version of events doing the rounds, to the effect that one of the other players hit David and Fergie took the rap but, given that David and Victoria laid the blame so firmly at Fergie's door, it seems unlikely.)

From that moment on, it was not a case of if but when. Various Spanish and Italian clubs had been sniffing around David for some time now and they all saw a possibility to land their prey. Real Madrid lost no time in putting feelers out, although they initially denied rumours that they wanted Beckham on board. Questioned in March about his intentions, Real Madrid President Florentino Perez attempted to dampen speculation, saying, 'I don't want to raise hopes and then he can't come here. He is a great player but we will not sign everyone on the market.' It was not, however, an outright denial and just one week later Real's managing director, Jorge Valdano, admitted, 'Beckham looks like the next big project for us.'

Sir Alex Ferguson also wanted to keep a lid on the gossip and, in April, he said, 'It is totally out of the question. There is no way we would sell him.' The person who threw doubt on that, though, was David himself, who appeared to be making discreet enquiries about the quality of life in Madrid. Fellow player and United goalkeeper Ricardo revealed, 'When I asked him if he was going to Real this summer, he started asking me questions about the quality of primary schools in Madrid.'

On 14 May, David was offered a new contract by United. The club did not want to repeat the wrangling over his contract that had happened the last time around and nor did they want David to be free to walk away when the current contract expired in two years' time. There was a meeting between Tony Stephens and Peter Kenyon at Old Trafford, when the new terms were laid out on the table – and they were not generous. David would have been offered only a £7,000-a-week pay rise – a fortune to most people, but not a lot when you're already on £95,000 a week. In total, it would have been a rise of £364,000 a year on a salary that was already £5 million. David suspected that the offer was deliberately low in order to tempt him to leave. Manchester United denied it.

'When we sat down with Sir Alex in May, it was the manager's view that, in order to continue the development of our team, we needed to make some changes on the playing side, which meant bringing some new players in to the squad,' said Peter Kenyon after it was all over. 'When making long-term plans on the playing side, we also review the age profile of our squad and, crucially, the status of key players' contracts. Normally, when a player has two years left on his contract, we either renew his deal or accept that it might be better if he moved on elsewhere, allowing us to earn a fee on his sale.

'What does not make sense for the club is to let top players leave the club at the end of their contract on a free transfer. In David's case, our approach in mid-May to his advisers about extending his current deal, which had just two years to run, did not meet with a positive response. We knew David was excited about the possibility of playing abroad and we felt that, if we could generate a substantial fee in a transfer deal, it would support our efforts to strengthen the squad for the next season.'

And in any case, Stephens had held private meetings with Real, AC Milan and Inter Milan in

April. Aware of the way the wind was blowing, David was getting his advisers to test the real level of interest in him out there.

Matters deteriorated yet further in April during a match against, ironically, Real Madrid. Ferguson left David on the bench during the first half of the Champions League game and he was not brought on until the second half, as a 63rd-minute substitute. He promptly went on to score two goals and appeared nearly in tears at the end of the match as he threw out his arms in a gesture of acknowledgement to the fans. Some interpreted it as a farewell gesture; many more felt that Ferguson was now allowing personal antipathy to get in the way of his own judgement. Whatever the truth, that was the moment that David had clearly had enough. He had been with Manchester United for 11 years and was also England captain. He did not merit treatment like that.

And so it was that David, Victoria and Tony Stephens met that night at Manchester's Malmaison Hotel to discuss the future. David's father Ted had already waded into the row, saying, 'After the game, David told me he was devastated about not being chosen. I think he should have played but I would say that, being his dad. Sir Alex usually gets things right. This time he got it wrong.'

Sir Alex, meanwhile, was suffering an onslaught from the press and was showing signs of pressure. Asked by a radio interviewer if he was sick of the hype surrounding Beckham, he screamed, 'You've been told not to fucking ask that. Cut that off. Cut that off. fucking idiots, you all are. You do that again and you won't be coming back here. You fucking sell your papers and radio stations on the back of this club.' There was a similar outburst to a reporter a few minutes later.

Real continued to insist that it was not interested in the player and David continued to play for United, eventually winning the Premiership 4–1 against Arsenal. David had scored in the game, but again appeared close to tears at the end, shaking hands and embracing his teammates. Poignantly, he stayed behind to kick a ball about with four-year-old Brooklyn, giving every appearance of showing his elder son the scene of past glories. It was very nearly time to say that final goodbye.

The whole team looked miserable that night as they gathered at Manchester's the Living Room. They were there to celebrate their victory, but David was already 200 miles away, back down in London. Pausing only to add two more tattoos to his already extensive collection and to buy a holiday home in the South of France, he and Victoria flew on to the United States. The newspaper *USA Today* had just carried a front-page picture of Beckham with the caption: 'The most famous athlete in all the world – except America'. If the Beckhams had anything to do with it, that was about to change. And so off they went, with the biggest change of all just a few weeks in the distance.

Even after the deal with Real was sewn up, fallout continued. In an interview with *Sports Illustrated* that was done before David's departure but published afterwards, Ferguson made it quite clear who he blamed for Beckham's transition from hard-working footballer to global icon. 'He was blessed with great stamina, the best of all the players I've had here,' he said. 'After training, he'd always be practising, practising, practising. But his life changed when he met his wife. She's in pop and David got another image. He developed this "fashion thing". I saw his transition to a different person.'

And even now, with the deal sewn up, David was clearly unhappy about the way he had been treated. 'It could have been handled a bit differently,' he said on his arrival in Tokyo later in the summer. 'I think things went on that obviously I wouldn't be happy about. I think, of course, it could have been done differently but I don't want to talk about that side of it because I'm a Real Madrid player now and I'm looking forward to it.'

He perked up and described the move as 'an exciting thing for the whole family. I haven't started [Spanish] lessons yet, but I know how to ask for the bill in a restaurant. If I was going to leave Manchester United at any time in my career then to join Real is a dream.'

And so he and Victoria set about moving the family to Madrid, as well as signing up with Simon Fuller, the Svengali behind the Spice Girls, with the hope of marketing themselves as a £1-billion global brand. And so here was David: rich, talented, successful, deliriously happily married, a doting father of two, world famous and signed up to the best football club in the world. Just how had it all gone so wrong?

Chapter Two

Baby Beckham

It was halfway through the 1970s, the decade that taste forgot. Harold Wilson was Prime Minister, the Bay City Rollers were top of the charts and the whole nation was wandering around in flares, wide collars and kipper ties. It was also the hottest summer for decades, inflation was rampant and Britain seemed set to decline gently into the status of a Third World country on the edge of Europe. And it was in the middle of this unlikely scenario that David Robert Joseph Beckham, style icon and national hero to be, was born.

David was actually born on 2 May 1975 in Whipps Cross Hospital in Leytonstone, east London, to Ted and Sandra, a kitchen fitter and a hairdresser. He was the second of three children – he has an older sister Lynne and a little sister Joanne – and soon after his birth the family moved to Chingford in Essex. Right from the start, it was clear that here was no ordinary infant. Practically from the moment he crawled from the cradle, Baby Becks was hooked on football, encouraged by his father, a massive Manchester United fan. The young Beckham was a good-looking boy. Early pictures show chubby cheeks and a cheeky smile, full of self-confidence. David's only problem, if you can call it that, was that he was fairly small; he was one of those boys who go through their childhood and teenage years shorter than their peers until the very last moment, when they shoot up. And so it was with David.

But football was a constant right from the start – and, unlike most young boys who love the sport and play as competent amateurs, David stood out. He not only loved it but he was proving fantastically good at it also. He would play wherever he was: at council football pitches near Ainsley Wood School, in Chingford, and on the flat surfaces near his grandparents' home nearby.

And David was truly dedicated. He would play alone, practising crossing the ball from the flanks into the penalty area, passing to open up the opposite team's defences and the dead-ball kicks that have made him famous throughout the world. Many believe he is now the world's best free-kick taker and it all stems from those hours and hours of practice as a child. It was astonishing dedication for a boy of seven, the age when he really began to take his football seriously. Other than that, he was a shy child, a trait that has stayed with him through adulthood.

Matthew Treglohan met David when the two attended Chase Lane Primary School and became firm friends with the young football devotee. 'We were all very quiet at school, David especially,' he later recalled. 'I used to sit next to him in geography and art classes. He was very good at art but was only ever really interested in football. He wasn't even that bothered about girls then. A few of the kids shone through in football, but Dave was certainly one of the best.'

After primary school, David moved on to Chingford School, where it soon became apparent he had a real talent for the game. After spotting an ad in a local paper, which read, 'Wanted: Football stars of the future', he began playing for a local team, the Ridgeway Rovers in the Enfield Sunday League, at what is now the Peter May Sports Ground in Wadham Road, Highams Park. There he distinguished himself by scoring over 100 goals in just three years. He also played for Chingford High, Waltham Forest District and Essex Under-15s.

'We were both 11 in our first proper football contest and David desperately wanted to start off with a goal,' said Nana Boachie, one of his schoolfriends, many years later. 'As goalie on the opposing side, I wanted to keep a clean sheet. He just said, "We'll see," in that quiet voice of his. Just before half-time, we gave away a free kick just outside the area. David curled the ball into the top corner. It was impossible to save. He still remembers it.' It was a sign of glories to come.

And, even at that young age, top clubs began to notice him, with both Arsenal and Tottenham Hotspur expressing an interest in the young protégé. But David wanted to play with Manchester United. It was his father's club and now David was a supporter of United, too. And it took some guts to stand up for his heroes: as a southerner, David was expected to support a southern team and later to play for one. To this day, there are some football fans who dislike David for what they see as his betrayal – playing for a Manchester club rather than a London one. But, back then, it was all still very harmless.

'I used to take so much stick from my mates at school,' David said. 'I had a couple of mates who were West Ham fans and a couple who were Tottenham or Arsenal fans. But I remember when we beat Arsenal 6–2 when Sharpey [Lee Sharpe] scored the hat-trick. I used to wear my United shirt over my school uniform on my way to school so I got a lot of stick, but I used to give a lot back.'

As he entered his teens, he had got himself a job as a potman at Walthamstow Dog Stadium, earning £10 a night, but it was clear by this time that David was a seriously talented football player and that is where his heart lay. It takes exceptional talent to become a professional football player but David had that talent, along with the drive and commitment to practise. All he ever wanted to do was to be a footballer – no other choice of career crossed his mind.

His first taste of kicking a ball at Old Trafford, home of Manchester United, came when he was only 11. He was competing in the 1986 TSB Bobby Charlton Soccer Skills final and won – the youngest competitor ever to do so. The prize was, ironically given his later career, a two-week trip to Spain to train with Barcelona, at that point managed by Terry Venables. The young David was ecstatic: he met the then heroes of the day, including Gary Lineker, Steve Archibald and Mark Hughes.

And the match also gave him his first taste of what it can be like to take abuse from the crowd. The final was just before a match with London club Tottenham Hotspur and so Tottenham fans were out in force. 'All the Spurs fans were there and, as I was doing the dribbling in and out of the cones, they announced that this was David Beckham of Essex,' he said later. 'The Spurs fans started singing and cheering, but then the announcer said I was a Man United fan. They booed me and I went into a couple of cones.'

It might have been the first time that David was subject to abuse from the crowd, but it certainly was not the last. Even in a sport noted for the harsh way in which it can treat its stars, David has stood out from the crowd. He may be the most loved footballer in

Britain but, in some cases, he is also the most loathed, not least because the fans are jealous. He has the looks, the talent, the Spice Girl and the cars – and some people cannot forgive him for it. In later years, it was only David's strength of character that enabled him to endure a kind of viciousness that no other star of his generation has had to put up with.

Back at school, though, David was not doing so well. He was not a natural academic and was much more interested in fooling around with his fellow students than he was in attending to his lessons. His school reports when he was aged 12 are extremely revealing. 'David is continually silly, which he cannot afford to be if he wishes to make progress,' snapped his French teacher. 'I can only hope for a more mature approach.'

Other teachers were no more impressed. 'His behaviour has been extremely silly,' said Home Economics. 'Could do a lot better.' 'David has ability but finds it difficult to concentrate,' worried Humanities. 'His attitude must improve immediately if he is to fulfil his potential.' Even Sports had a go. 'David has a natural ability to succeed at most sports,' his teacher observed. 'But he should be careful of distractions, which affect his application.' David himself was under no illusion as to his performance at school. 'I would have enjoyed lessons at school more if we'd talked about football,' he said. 'But I was quite good at art – maybe I'd have gone into that if I had not got my break into soccer.'

The trouble was that by now the boys in David's class were a rowdy lot and he got sucked in with it. And, while the boisterous side of his nature served him well as a sportsman, it didn't do a lot for him when it came to learning grammar. 'To be honest, teachers used to find David and his friends hard to control,' said one former master. 'He and six or seven of his cronies were together in the same class. They caused quite a few problems. The girls were very bright, very hard-working. But the boys wouldn't listen or pay attention. There'd be paper flicking and jostling around. David would be in the middle of that somewhere. They were boys straight out of a comic at times.'

But David's attitude on the football pitch was very different. Venables had been impressed – and he was not the only one. David went on to do a trial with Leyton Orient and a spell at Tottenham Hotspur's school of excellence, but it was United that he wanted to join – and now, finally, they wanted him too. Manchester United talent scout Malcolm Fidgeon was becoming increasingly impressed as he watched David's progress and matters came to a head when he was playing against Redbridge for the Waltham Forest Under-12s. Fidgeon was present. 'I leaped into the air and started to cry,' David recalled later, on learning that a talent scout from United was present.

'It was a dream come true. It was one of my best games for the district. Being from London and being a southerner, I never thought I would get seen by a scout of Man United. But then I was lucky enough one day and I had a good game for my district side. I remember getting changed and I walked out and my mum called me over – my dad was working. There was excitement in her voice when she said, "It's lucky you had a good game, because there was a scout here from Man United and he wants to talk to Dad to discuss taking you to the club for trials."'

David was over the moon. By this time it was already clear that he had the talent to be a professional footballer, but to be spotted by the club of his dreams was almost too much. Ted was equally delighted. Not only was he also a huge United fan, but the signing also came as a testament to his coaching skills. He was the first person to teach David how to play football and he was the first person who coached his talented son. The club finally signed David as a schoolboy associate on his 14th birthday. 'David is a good prospect,' said a spokesman for the club. 'We are delighted that he is joining us.'

The family was thrilled. 'But the best thing is, he is still a nice boy. He has not changed at all,' said a delighted Sandra. Nor was David letting any jealousy from friends get to him. 'Most people at school are very friendly, there are a couple of other lads who have signed for professional teams,' he said. 'Sometimes a player tries to kick you, but that's part of the game.' It was an attitude that was to be sorely tested in later years as David's star continued to rise – and attract much more than just schoolboy jealousy along the way.

The Manchester United youth coach at the time was Eric Harrison, who was responsible for bringing on some of the biggest talents in football. David was clearly talented anyway, but under the guidance of Harrison he was to start on the process that would turn him into one of the all-time greats. And Harrison was superb at his job. 'A good football coach is like a good schoolteacher – they realise the youngsters are the important ones,' he said. 'We do it for the kids, not for our own egos. I have taken so much pleasure from seeing young players develop both as footballers and people. David Beckham might have funny haircuts and live a different life from the rest of us, but the important thing is, he's a really good kid, as well.

'Respect was a word I used all the time to Beckham, Giggs and the other players at United. We as adult coaches respect the youngsters and in return the youngsters should also be respectful. I am a hard taskmaster and never let the kids at United step out of line or become arrogant. Players should be confident, yes, but not arrogant where they think they know it all.' His attitude worked. Of all the many things David has been accused of over the years, arrogance has never been one of them. He has always acknowledged the skills and talents of others, always thanked his coaches and teammates when thanks were due and, in as much as a global icon can be modest, still retains an air of modesty even now that he has reached the very top.

Back then, all David could think about was football. He was a natural sportsman, winning the Essex 1,500-metre championship four years in a row, a talent that only added to his footballing prowess. And he was determined to succeed. This determination gave him an edge: many boys would like to be footballers, but not many would give up going to the pub, girlfriends and all the general chaos that teenage life involves. David did. Rather than hanging out with other boys after school, he would be back to the football pitch to practise for hours – just like Victoria, incidentally, who gave up her after-school hours learning how to dance. In both cases, it paid off.

'I gave up a lot when I was younger,' David once said, 'going out with the lads, parties and discos, leaving my family. It wasn't easy, but I knew it was what I wanted to do. I used to tell everyone and they'd laugh and say, "Yeah, but what else you gonna do?" I'd say, "No, football." United was the dream.'

It was a dream that he made clear to everyone. He was still working part-time at the stadium, where he met Joe Kinnear, then manager of Wimbledon, who, spotting his talent, tried to lure him to Wimbledon's home, Selhurst Park. David turned him down as he was by now absolutely determined to be a United player. 'Beckham must have been about 15,' Kinnear recalled. 'He was a quiet lad but was obviously mad on football and I wanted him. But he told me he had his heart set on going to Old Trafford.'

34

And something else was happening in David's life: girls were beginning to notice him. He had always been a good-looking little boy but, as he began to grow slightly taller and more muscular, it was not only his footballing talents that attracted attention. He was a natural charmer and his shyness only added to the overall appeal. 'He would blush if someone teased him,' said Diane Gleeson, a regular at the track. 'One lady customer took a real shine to him and told him it was time he found out what it was like to spend a night with a good woman. David said, "Yes, I'd love to come round to your place after work. Can I bring my mum and dad?"'

Of course, he never took her up on the offer. His first love was football and he simply didn't have time for a girlfriend on top of the hours of practice he continued to put in. Indeed, for someone who is a heart-throb on top of everything else he's famous for, David has had surprisingly few girlfriends and the only one who was ever serious was Victoria.

But that single-minded determination was to stand him in very good stead. So was a certain maturity that distinguished him and made him stand out from the crowd from the very beginning. David does have a short-tempered streak when playing football, which was to get him into terrible trouble, but he was also notable for his maturity from a very young age. It was this that made his relationship with Victoria become so serious so quickly, and this that has made him able to cope with his fame. It was also this that gave him the strength he needed to leave home when he was just 16. For David, a southerner by birth and by upbringing, it was time to move up north.

Chapter Three

The Boy Done Good

When David first moved to Manchester at the tender age of 16, he was lucky in his choice of lodgings. After a couple of digs – David had to leave the first when a fellow player misbehaved and the second after he criticised the food – he ended up living with Annie and Tommy Kay, a couple in their 70s, who provided lodgings for about 50 Manchester United players over more than 30 years. The couple live next to The Cliff in Salford, which at the time was Manchester United's training ground, and David spent four years with his 'surrogate grandparents'.

And the young Man U player was concerned about his appearance even then. 'When David first came, I never thought this could be the future England captain,' says Annie, who now has grandchildren of her own.

'Having said that, he was always dedicated and a very smart dresser. When he came with his clothes he brought seven bags – most young footballers just had two. I said, "You've got some bags!" He said, "I've got some more!" He was very clothes-conscious even when he was 16 and stood out in the neighbourhood. The girls loved him but he wasn't bothered. He'd always be very friendly and always talk but he was very keen on his football. There was not much time for girlfriends.

'Victoria has improved him a bit but he was very fashion-conscious before he ever met her. He was never a slob. He was always picky and he'd sort his own room out – he said, "Give me my bedding and I'll change my bed." There wasn't a thing out of place in his room. Not like some of the others we've had here. I'd give Mark Hughes his shirts and everything and he'd drop them on the floor. I'd pick them up but he'd say, "I know where everything is if it's on the floor."'

Beckham himself remembers the time with a good deal of fondness. 'My third home in Manchester is the one that holds the greatest affection,' he recalled in his autobiography. 'It was the home in Lower Broughton of the terrific Annie and Tommy Kay. Mark Hughes, a legend in my eyes, stayed in the room that I had for a number of years. It was just like being an addition to their own family and they looked after me brilliantly – and the great thing, especially for a teenager, was that they allowed me to have my space.'

Although the room has the words 'Gillian's Room'

on the door, because it once belonged to one of the couple's two children, the Kays have left it exactly as it was in David's day. Inside is a clock, a copper-coin collection, a Union Flag towel and a toy gorilla bearing the words 'I love you' – it was presented to David by a mystery admirer. There is also a slightly deflated football – and a full-length mirror.

'This was the one place he wanted to come to because Mark Hughes was here and he was his hero,' says Annie. 'The club wanted him to come to us as he was a very good prospect. What a prospect! I didn't know he had the talent then, but he has something special. He lived and breathed football and never got injured. Every time David sees me [now] he says, "Annie, you must come to the house." I say, "I've seen it in *OK! Magazine*."'

Other players also remember a style-conscious young man. 'He's always been a flash cockney,' fellow player Ryan Giggs once said. 'Even at 17 when we all had Honda Preludes, he had a leather interior and a personalised licence plate.' Gary Neville, who was to become David's best friend and best man at his wedding to Victoria, remembers something similar. 'I still remember coming across him in the youth teams,' he said in an interview with *The Times*. 'All of us local lads, such as Nicky Butt, me and Paul Scholes, wondered who this flash cockney lad was. He always used to have the latest United tracksuit and the club clearly rated him.'

David loved his new life and set about training with gusto, earning the princely sum of £29.50 a week plus a tenner for expenses (the rate went up when they hit 17). And he certainly had an apprenticeship to serve. Man U expected its trainees to do jobs around the club, including serving in Man U's shop and cleaning the boots belonging to older players. It was a life that was very different from the one Beckham lives now.

And it was not until 1992, a year after he joined Man U as a trainee, that he made his debut in the League Cup tie against Brighton as a substitute for Andrei Kanchelskis in a match that ended 1–1 – four months before he signed his professional contract. The Class of 1992 – aka 'Fergie's Fledglings' – has gone down in footballing history: the team also contained Ryan Giggs, Paul Scholes, Nicky Butt and the Neville brothers.

Alex Ferguson, for one, was only too aware of the mass of talent he had in his hands. 'There are more like Keith [Gillespie] in our youth team and we are looking closely at them,' he said in an interview in January 1993, just after Gillespie's sensational debut in a match against Bury and a few months after the team had won the FA Youth Cup. 'We don't like to go overboard about young players, but this lot are very exciting. With their ability and desire to play, they should go far. Winning the FA Youth Cup can be significant. When United last won it in 1964, it triggered the best period in the club's post-Munich history.'

In another interview given a few days later, he went

even further. 'These boys are the best crop I have had in my management career,' he said. 'We have 18 trainees and every one of them will be given a full professional contract at 18. We don't have any doubt about them making their mark in the game. To have them all come through like this is very rare. Now it's just a matter of fitting them into the first team when the opportunity arises.'

Indeed, the up-and-coming boys were so well thought of that they actually enhanced Sir Alex's reputation. 'People say Alex should be handed the Old Trafford manager's job for life if he brings us the title this season for the first time in 26 years,' said footballing legend Bobby Charlton, now a director of United. 'But he already has the job for as long as he wants it. He deserves it for all the work he has put in at Old Trafford in the last six years and not just with the first team. What really impresses me about Manchester United under Alex's management is not the way the first team are playing – it's the future that fills me with such confidence.

'Of course, we fancy our chances of taking the title this season. It's going to be either us, Aston Villa or Blackburn. But I fancy our chances just as strongly in the FA Youth Cup, which we won last season. We are already in the fourth round against Wimbledon and I'm certain we'll go all the way again. That's how highly I rate the kids Alex has brought into the club.

'I've never known us – or any club in England – to

have so many potentially brilliant youngsters. We have so many we are actually having to turn some very talented teenagers away. When I see these kids, I get really excited. They are an absolute joy, the way they play. Five or six of this year's youth team are certain to figure in the Premier League in the next couple of seasons. They are already that good. And it's all down to Alex Ferguson.'

Surprisingly, perhaps, David's career did not take off immediately and for some time he feared it would not take off at Old Trafford at all. He was a slow developer. He turned professional in 1993 and scored in his Champions League debut against Galatasaray in 1994, but experienced what he wrongly thought would be a career hiccup in early 1995. Sir Alex Feguson, Manchester United's redoubtable manager, called Beckham into his office in February 1995 and told him he was going on a month's loan to Preston. He was devastated. 'I definitely didn't want to go – and that's nothing against Preston. I was gutted really because I felt my career was over at Manchester United,' he said later. 'The manager assured me it wasn't and it's the best thing I've ever done in my career going to Preston. I scored straight from a corner on my debut and from a free kick in my second game, so things went quite well.'

Gary Neville, by now very close to Beckham, was aware of his friend's feelings. 'I knew he was worried,' he said. 'He thought that was the end of him at United.

We all knew he had great ability but people said he was a bit soft going into tackles and headers. Going in to the Third Division with Preston and having people kick lumps out of him toughened him up.'

During his time with the club, David began to show serious promise. He made five league appearances and scored twice – including the first of his famous free kicks. But, although he was clearly turning out to be an exceptional talent, there were no openings in the team – until Ferguson decided it was time to make use of his new talent.

He had been nurturing the Class of '92 for four years and now he wanted them out on the field. He thus sold Kanchelskis, Paul Ince and Mark Hughes – and the Class of '92 was on its way. Beckham could not believe his luck. 'When I was coming through the ranks, I didn't see any light at the end of the tunnel for me because there was Andrei who was flying,' he said later. 'Then, all of a sudden, the door opened when the manager sold them and got us youngsters in.' Ironically, of course, it never occurred to David that one day the same fate would await him.

Nor were many onlookers impressed. Ex-footballer and pundit Alan Hansen commented on *Match of the Day*, 'You can't win anything with kids.' It was a view shared by many in the field – although it was not long before they were proven wrong.

In April Beckham returned to Man U and quickly began to show his true form. He made his Premier

League debut at home to Leeds United on 2 April 1995 and it was in the following season, 1995/6, that he really began to distinguish himself. He was playing predominantly in the right midfield position that had once been held by Kanchelskis and began to show his form, scoring the winning goal in the FA Cup semi-final against Chelsea. Man U won its second double at the end of that season. It was a taste of what was to come.

But, despite all David's early promise, he was a tortoise rather than a hare. It was not until August 1996 that he finally began to stand out from the rest of the hugely talented Class of '92 when Manchester United played Wimbledon at Selhurst Park and he scored what is still one of his most famous goals, beating Neil Sullivan from just inside his own half. 'It changed my life,' David later recalled. 'The ball seemed to be in the air for hours and it all went quiet. Then the ball went in and it just erupted. I was on cloud nine. I just wanted to shake everyone's hand and stay out on the pitch for half an hour.'

He was right: it did change his life. The following month the then England manager Glenn Hoddle handed David his first cap against Moldova in a World Cup qualifier, marking the start of his international career. He went on to play in all the World Cup qualifying games and by the end of the 1996/7 season had won the PFA Young Player of the Year, come second in the Player of the Year voting, won two league titles and reached the European Cup semifinals. Manchester United, meanwhile, went on to win the Premiership and FA Cup double in 1996. It was heady stuff for a young man who was still only 21 but David showed a degree of maturity beyond his years.

'You cannot afford to let things go to your head,' he said at the time. 'First of all you'd get hammered by the other lads, then you have to face up to the boss. The first sign that you're getting carried away and he comes down like a ton of bricks. I know how difficult it's been just breaking into the first team and I'm not going to do anything to put that at risk. On the pitch sometimes it's beyond your control, but off it's down to you and I would be stupid to think I'm something special.

'Anyway, how can someone as inexperienced as me try to be big-time when I look at the players alongside me? They've probably forgotten more than I'll ever know. People like Peter Schmeichel, Eric Cantona and Gary Pallister have won just about everything going – and all I've done is scratch the surface. Hopefully, in a few years I will be able to sit back and think I've achieved something, but at the moment I'm just struggling to hold down a first-team place.'

Everyone was waking up to quite what a fine player they had on their hands. Graham Rix, the man chosen by Hoddle to oversee the fledglings, was vastly impressed. 'Different class,' he said at the time. 'You can look at players of that age and tell the ones who will fail and who will make it, and those who will be stars. Becks is going to be a true star. Everybody knows what he can do with a ball at his feet, but that's not as important as what goes on away from game situations. Tell him something in training and it's done instantly; ask him to do something and there's no moans, raised eyebrows or questions, he just gets on with it.

'A manager or coach is always looking for somebody who can take what they demand on to the pitch and impart it to the other players. Tony Adams is the perfect example – a manager in player's kit – and I think that is what Becks will develop into. He's still learning his trade but give him five years and I think Alex Ferguson will regard him as his general.'

As it happens, it didn't take five years. Beckham was learning fast, not least because Steve Bruce, the former United captain, had just left to go to Liverpool. It forced his erstwhile teammates to grow up fast. 'To have somebody like Steve in the dressing room was a blessing for all the youngsters,' Beckham said at the time. 'He was a father figure, the person we could all turn to if there was something wrong. I was very close to him. He'd helped sort out a few problems I'd had and, with his advice, I think I came out stronger, a better person as well as player. Now he's not here, we will have to learn how to stand on our own feet. There are other players you can talk to, obviously, but Brucie was a bit special when it came to giving the kids a boost. It's strange not having him around.'

However, Eric Cantona was still around and he was proving an inspiration to the young players. 'You can't put into words what Eric means to us,' said Beckham. 'Just having him out on the pitch wearing a red shirt is more of a boost than you could ever explain. Other teams are frightened of him, I'm convinced of that. They know how dangerous he can be and that is worth a goal start to us.

'He's also been brilliant with the young players. He doesn't say too much, stand up at the blackboard and give us coaching lessons or anything, but a simple word of advice now and again often means more than a thousand coaching sessions. You only play with people like that once in your career. My hero was Bryan Robson. I wasn't around when he was at his best, but I'm just as proud to say I played in the same team as Eric Cantona.'

Beckham's modesty knew no bounds. Apart from praising his teammates, he was not letting anything go to his head and, despite Man U's phenomenal performance in the 1995/6 season, he knew that he still had to prove himself over and again. 'Winning the double means nothing this season,' he said at the beginning of the 1996/7 season. 'It's great to look at a couple of medals, but if we don't win anything this year, the hard work we put in last season counts for nothing. The fact that a lot of us were so young when we first tasted success doesn't mean we lose any hunger – there's no way the boss would let that happen. Winning is a great feeling. The more you get it, the more you want it.'

And, he was asked, would he ever like to be England captain? Becks was circumspect. 'I would be lying if I didn't look at Gary and Phil Neville during the summer and say I wasn't jealous of them being in the full squad,' he said, managing to be as charming and modest as ever, even while confessing to jealousy. 'But I was privileged to captain the Under-21s and I just have to accept it has taken me longer to make the step up than Gary or Phil. I'm not going to sulk – being part of any England set-up is a dream come true. I just hope I get the chance to make my mark on the full squad.' That wish was to be fulfilled.

Girls did play a part in his life, although not a very big one. He dated Leoni Marzell from Essex for a year but, although she called him a 'fantastic lover', his primary interest was elsewhere. 'He'd rather talk about Arsenal all night with my dad than enjoy a bedroom romp with me,' she said, although after David's engagement she went on to say, 'Deep down he is everything a girl could want. Posh is very lucky.' Other girlfriends were Anna Bartley, a former Miss Wales, who went out with David for two and a half years and Julie Killilea. There was also the odd fling, but nothing serious – for now.

And so David went on until mid 1997, racking up one success after another, making his name in the game and more than fulfilling the predictions of greatness. But he was about to step into another world. Although well known in footballing circles, David was still a long way away from superstardom and his status as one of the most famous men in the world. All that was about to change, for in mid-1997 he met a woman who was going to turn his life upside down. Her name was Victoria Adams.

Chapter Four

Posh and Becks

Victoria Caroline Adams was born in Harlow, Essex, on 17 April 1974, the oldest of three children. Her parents, Tony and Jackie, ran a successful electrical wholesalers and, when Victoria was still young, the family moved to Goff's Oak in Hertfordshire – where they were the only family with their own swimming pool.

Like her future husband, Victoria was born ambitious and also like David, she began to pursue her dream in early childhood. She loved to dance and had done so since she was a toddler – 'I did some shows when I was very young – two or three,' she later recalled. 'When I was about eight, I did one where I was dressed up in a bright-yellow top hat and tails with sequins all over it, yellow fishnet tights and yellow tap shoes with yellow tap bows. I danced to "If My Friends Could See Me Now", that Shirley MacLaine song from *Sweet Charity* – and I was Shirley MacLaine.'

By mid-1997, Victoria was a superstar – far more famous than David. The Spice Girls had sprung seemingly out of nowhere the previous year, and were in the process of taking over the world. And it was as a Spice Girl that David first encountered his bride-to-be. In January 1997, David had been abroad with the England team when a Spice Girls video appeared on the television in the room he was sharing with Gary Neville. It was for the song 'Say You'll Be There', in which Victoria, billed as Midnight Miss Suki, spent the entire time dancing around in black leather. Becks sat up. 'That's the girl for me,' he told a bemused Gary. 'I'm going to get her.' He later recalled, 'I was watching the Spice Girls on TV and I knew instantly she was the one for me. She is everything I want in a person.'

Unbeknown to him, Victoria had also been attracted to David before they'd even met: shown a series of pictures of footballers by a magazine and asked to pick the most attractive, she picked David. 'In December 1996, I was interviewing the Spice Girls,' said the writer Juliette Wills. 'I'd brought along a few pictures of footballers to see if the girls fancied any of them. Mel C had a thing for Jamie Redknapp. Mel B was too busy shouting and eating sausages to look. Emma was smoking a fag and Geri was fiddling with her lipstick. So I asked Victoria to go through the photos.

'Victoria was apparently uninterested in Lee Sharpe, Denis Irwin and Iain Dowie before coming to a picture of one David Beckham. "Who's he?" she said, blushing. "He's lovely."

"That's David Beckham," I said.

"Is he famous?" she giggled, holding the photo in her lap.

"A bit. He's pretty good at football," I said. "Do you fancy him?"

'She stood up, adjusted her short, suede skirt and nodded. Like a woman possessed she said, "I'm going to ask him out to dinner."'

And so it was that in March 1997 Victoria jumped at the chance to accompany fellow Spice Girl Melanie Chisholm – Sporty Spice – to a match at Old Trafford. No one was aware of the momentous implications of this match. 'Manchester United, appropriately enough in front of the Spice Girls Mel C and Victoria, showed the rest of the Premiership that the other teams are in danger of remaining frustrated wannabes,' wrote Matt Dickinson in the *Sunday Express*. The headline was 'Cole goal adds Spice to the Premiership race', but other than that there was no further mention of the future Mrs B.

The crowd booed Mel, who supported Liverpool, which in turn alerted David to the fact that there was someone famous in the crowd. He asked a fellow player who it was – a couple of Spice Girls, said the fellow player. 'I jumped up and said, 'Which ones?

Which ones?' David later recalled. 'But whoever said it couldn't remember. And it was a struggle to get my mind back on the match.'

Victoria, meanwhile, was having trouble working out which player was Beckham – she couldn't see properly because she'd forgotten to bring her glasses.

The game over – Man U beat Sheffield Wednesday 2–0 – David and his fellow teammates retired to the players' bar. Victoria and Mel were already in situ, with Victoria, by her own admission, a little tipsy. And now, with his big chance to talk to the object of his desires, David did nothing. He was too shy to approach her. It was Victoria who had to seize the moment: she marched over to him and demanded, 'Good game?' It had been love even before first sight for both of them – feelings that were strengthened just by that one glance. And now it was the real thing. 'I do believe in love at first sight and from our first meeting I knew he was the man I wanted to spend the rest of my life with,' Victoria said later.

Having finally met, the two of them really clicked, not least as David explained that the attractive blonde he had been talking to was his sister Joanne. 'I could see he was shy,' Victoria said afterwards. 'I found that really attractive.'

David, meanwhile, was delighted to have made Posh drop the trademark pout. 'As soon as she smiled I knew everything was going to be OK.' he said.

Steve Aspey, a decorator, was present at the time. 'It

really was a case of "Their eyes met across a crowded room",' he said in an interview in 2000. 'Proper love at first sight. Posh spotted Becks looking at her and made a beeline straight for him. After that, they were totally wrapped up in each other. It was lovely. You could tell Becks was extremely nervous in the crowded Old Trafford players' bar. She and Mel C were getting loads of attention. But all the time Victoria was looking around as if she wanted to see someone in particular. With hindsight she was on the lookout for Becks.

'He arrived and got a pint of orange juice. Posh was drinking red wine and marched straight over to him. I asked them both if they would mind having their photo taken with my 14-year-old lad Paul. They were super to him and agreed straight away. But it was obvious that they just wanted to be left alone. The packed room could have been completely deserted as far as they were concerned. They just kept looking into one another's eyes.

'Posh was a bit chubbier than she is these days. She even had a bit of a double chin. But she still looked fantastic in an unbuttoned blouse that showed her bra. I could see Becks eyeing her up and down as she did most of the talking. Then they swapped phone numbers – and their love affair had started.'

In fact, David had said, 'Well I was wondering, Victoria, if you weren't doing anything after the game, I mean, perhaps we could have dinner?' Victoria was doing something so David said he'd give her a ring. 'You better,' the Spice Girl replied.

Beckham later recalled that he refused to give her his number in case she didn't call, dashed home and wrote Victoria's number on six different pieces of paper to be sure not to lose it, then tentatively rang to make the first date. The pair met in an Essex car park and first went to a Chinese restaurant but, when they discovered that neither of them could eat as they weren't hungry, they ended up at Mel C's flat – in a room covered in pictures of Liverpool.

Victoria was off the next day for a short trip to New York, but the pair promised to keep in touch by phone and so, on her return a week later, the two had already been chatting for hours. Victoria had also dealt with another minor problem hovering in the background – her boyfriend, Stuart Bilton. From the moment she and David first met, neither of them had any doubt at all that they were made for each other, and so Stuart was given his marching orders and the two began dating in earnest.

The unlikely fairy godmother – or godfather – was Simon Fuller, the Spice Girls' manager. He had been keen for Victoria to go out with a footballer, thinking it would bolster the girls' image still further, and had tried unsuccessfully to persuade Victoria to attend a number of football games before that final, fateful match. Victoria was having none of it – until she saw the chance to meet David. Now, however, with his wishes fulfilled, Fuller began to get worried that the publicity might be almost too much. Victoria was in no mood to listen. 'Who wants to be sensible when you're falling in love?' she said. 'And already I had a quivery feeling I was.'

David and Victoria were soon absolutely besotted with each other, but at first the relationship blossomed slowly. Remembering her opening line of 'Good game?' Victoria said, 'He laughed and that was it – even though for the first three dates he was so shy he didn't kiss me. He finally got round to it when we were at my parents' house after our fourth date. It was worth the wait.'

At first, the pair tried to keep it a secret but this soon proved impossible. The Spice Girls were at the height of their fame and their every move was avidly seized upon – especially when David and Victoria were spotted dancing together in a nightclub. Rumours began to circulate that she had taken him to meet her parents and Victoria's mother did nothing to squash the speculation when she said brightly, 'Everything in her life is wonderful at the moment. She's on top of the world. We've been told not to talk about David.'

Before long it was apparent that the couple had a great deal in common. Although Victoria's family was much wealthier than David's, the two had had similar childhoods – a single-minded obsession with succeeding in the chosen fields, which stood them in very good stead in adulthood. Now that they were adults, they had more frivolous similarities too – not least a love of fashion. David caused a furore when he appeared wearing Gucci loafers with no socks – this was before the days of Mohicans, sarongs, modelling contracts and so forth – causing Victoria to blurt out: 'This is what I've always said, "If you wanna be my lover, wear a pair of Gucci loafers." I do like a man who dresses well.' She'd found one.

Sightings of the two became increasingly frequent. After a game against Newcastle, Becks was seen slinking away from the post-match celebrations to be with Victoria. Then they were spotted kissing in the garden of David's Cheshire home. Victoria's mother added fuel to the fire. 'David is a wonderful young man and he treats Victoria very well,' she said. 'They see quite a lot of each other, despite the fact that they both have very hectic lives. Of course, David would be welcomed into our family. He is such a decent guy. I couldn't ask more for my daughter. There's been a lot of speculation about Victoria and David but the future really is up to them.'

Victoria later recalled the early days. 'I fancied David long before we met,' she said. 'I wasn't attracted by his fame but, as we got to know each other, we realised it was a great bonus. We are equally famous and attract equal attention. We're in the same boat and that brought us together very quickly. We used to go out in disguises – hats, glasses, all sorts of ridiculous clothes.'

The relationship had by now become really serious.

In June, David admitted what everyone already knew: that they were an item and, when their schedules meant they couldn't be together, they spoke to each other every day on the phone. 'That's normal,' he went on. 'I'm a footballer and she is a Spice Girl. It would be silly if we did not think the media and public were attracted to us. But we are just two normal young people going out together.

'It helps that Victoria is famous. It helps with the pressure if she is involved because we both share it. We do understand the pressure, even though we are only 22 and 23. We are learning together. I don't see myself as front-page news but going out with Victoria I am going to get it. It is something we must handle.'

It was an attitude that was going to prove crucial to David's mental well-being. They didn't know it yet, but the attention Posh and Becks were attracting was practically nothing compared to what was yet to come.

Not everyone was delighted, though. Football commentators grumbled that all the attention was bad for the game and that David couldn't have both a high-profile relationship and a successful career – and it is a mark of quite how unusual a man and a footballer David is that he has so emphatically proved them wrong. Meanwhile pop commentators were also muttering darkly, this time about Victoria. The Spice Girls had an extremely arduous schedule, taking them out of the country for many months at a time, and, as the bond between David and Victoria deepened, those separations were becoming increasingly difficult to bear. Would Victoria leave the group, asked the pundits?

David himself admitted that it could be difficult. 'I miss her so much when we're apart,' he said, adding, 'She's busy filming the Spice Girls' movie at the moment, so we get very little time together – and that's hard.'

As David's profile soared, so too did his earning potential. Brylcreem signed him up in a £1-million deal to endorse the product – and, unsurprisingly, the ensuing press conference saw a good many questions about David's relationship. 'I have never discussed with Victoria what her favourite sort of Brylcreem is,' he said wearily, 'so I just don't know.' And would he wear it on his wedding day? Becks just giggled. 'Yes, he will,' said Brylcreem executive Kay Downs.

David's fellow footballers were in two minds about it all. 'Some of the lads have been giving me stick over it but I really don't mind,' David confided.

It was the start of David's progress to becoming a seriously wealthy man. He was by now earning £10,000 a week and was increasingly seen wearing a Cartier watch (a present from Victoria) and dressing in Gucci. David spoke warily of the pitfalls of his new high profile. 'I know dating Victoria has doubled the media interest in me,' he said. 'We like to go for quiet meals together, but we always seem to be photographed shopping. I sometimes think people must think I live in Gucci and Prada shops. I worry that fans will forget I play football as well as go out with a Spice Girl. But I've turned down a lot of sponsorship offers because I want to be known as a footballer.'

The couple had only been together for four months, but both clearly knew that this was it. In the latest instalment of the real-life soap opera, they were spotted looking at houses together. A wedding announcement seemed imminent. There was only one fly in the ointment – Alex Ferguson.

Sir Alex Ferguson's antagonism to David's relationship with Victoria is not a recent development: it was there right from the very beginning. David had come to regard Ferguson as a second father, while Ferguson saw David as a supremely gifted player, not only talented but also willing to dedicate himself entirely to the game. Victoria represented a shift in emphasis. Although he had had other girlfriends, this was the first time in his life that David appeared to think of something – their relationship – as equally, if not more, important than football. Victoria's presence also changed the relationship between Fergie and Becks. Now there was someone else with an influential role in his life, who could hold sway over David and who had her own very determined ideas about the way he should live his life. And Sir Alex didn't like it one bit.

And so he did what he was to do time and again in the future: he punished David through his football. In August 1997, Ferguson sent his brilliant young player to play in a friendly at Bournemouth and dropped him from the Wembley clash with Chelsea, while making it clear that he disapproved of the publicity surrounding the relationship and casting doubts on David's fitness to play. The footballing world was aghast at the perceived insult to the rising hero.

'David is a world-class player and this is an insult to him,' said former United manager Tommy Docherty. 'I think the young man has handled himself superbly. Ferguson says that you take a long-term view on players. It's lucky that Brazil didn't take a long-term view on Pele. Beckham has been an absolute model pro. He's a good lad and this decision doesn't make any sense. He's 21, he should be fit for everything.'

David scored to take Bournemouth to a 1–0 win and Ferguson softened enough to say that he would consider playing David in the next day's Charity Shield, but remained unrepentant about what he had done. 'I was concerned about the tournament at the end of the last season in France,' he said. 'There is a price to pay for it. Gary Neville admitted to me that he felt really tired before he even went there.

'As far as David is concerned, we are fortunate in having a tremendous midfield of Paul Scholes, Nicky Butt and Roy Keane. I can add David when I feel the time is right, in two or three weeks. I believe we're doing the right thing for him. He is still immature as a player. He has still got a frame to fill – he will add a few more pounds. He is a later developer than some of the other young players. We will keep an eye on him.'

It was a very tough, uncompromising stance – and one that David was to encounter over and over throughout his years with United. With hindsight, it is possible to see that this tiny little crack in their relationship was the first chink that would ultimately lead to a fully blown rift.

Back then, though, Ferguson's intransigence merely looked like a passing phase, such as he displayed in a Champions League semi-final at Borussia Dortmund, when he told David to put his mobile phone away and stop talking to his girlfriend. The game ended in a 1–0 defeat. And so, after the friendly, it was back to business as usual, with reports that David had bought a new £70,000 Porsche (at Victoria's instigation), that she was spotted staying overnight at his Cheshire home – and even, amazingly enough, that Ferguson had had a brief change of heart and would be happy for the couple to wed, thinking that tabloid interest might then die down. Some hope …

Meanwhile, David was now attracting flak when he was out on the field, as rival fans taunted him about his girlfriend. Ferguson was supportive but firm. 'Top players will always get that kind of stick, but they grow up at Manchester United knowing it's the price they may have to pay for playing here,' he said. 'The entire team get stick, but some players take more than others and now David is under the spotlight. He is getting quite a bit of abuse, but he just has to handle it like Ryan Giggs has and like Mark Hughes and Eric Cantona did when they were here.' David did, in fact, behave impeccably: when taunted by Everton supporters after he had scored a goal, David held out his ear to invite a response from Man U fans – which he got.

By this time, less than six months into the relationship, rumours were beginning to circulate that the couple had married in private. Victoria was seen sporting a ring on her wedding finger, but assured the fans that it was of no consequence. Beckham, meanwhile, was worrying about the next season and confided, 'That [the last season] was the best of my career, so I've sat down with my dad and the manager to talk abut how to keep it at that level. We all feel I can still get better. Alex Ferguson told me to rest a lot, practise a lot, look after myself and, most importantly, just concentrate on my football and nothing else.' It was a forlorn hope. David continued to maintain that football was the most important thing in his life but there was no question that that position was now shared with Victoria.

As the 1997/8 season got under way, even calm, level-headed David began to show some signs of stress. He responded to taunts about Victoria by screaming and waving his fists at West Ham supporters, although he did manage to calm down when told off by the referee. Matters were not helped when Victoria appeared on LWT's *Spice Up Your Life* and cheerfully admitted she knew nothing about football.

The fans weren't pleased but, as David and

Victoria's relationship went from strength to strength, the two seemed to grow even closer in the face of opposition. A very high-pressure lifestyle and relationship can either make or break a relationship and there is no doubt in this case that it was the former. Both were famous, both had come under pressure before they met one another and now both helped the other cope with the price of fame.

'Victoria is used to the fame and all the adulation. We talk about it a lot. That helps,' said David. 'Football has become like showbusiness, which is something everybody in the game will have to contend with. When you're a kid, all you want is to play football – you don't anticipate everything that comes with it, like the sponsorship deals and all the fame and people noticing you when you're out. You have to understand how people are and what you are to them. I am still coming to terms with it, but I will be able to cope.

'We take every opportunity to enjoy our privacy. We'd like a little more. But we know we are high-profile people. It would be the same for me whatever I did because of Victoria's business. We would like to lead normal lives and do things that don't get noticed. But I have put myself in that situation by what I am doing on the field. Now it is a case of dealing with what happens off it.'

Even so, David's life was not one of unqualified bliss. Despite the happiness he'd found with Victoria, life could be lonely at times, especially because the couple's busy schedules meant that they were often apart. It is difficult to remember the furore that greeted the Spice Girls these days but, back then, three years before the turn of the millennium, they were briefly some of the most famous women on the planet. And while Victoria was racing all over the world, David remained at his home in Cheshire.

'I go for a lot of meals on my own,' he revealed. 'In the local Chinese they know me, so they sit me in the corner out of the way and I order what I want as quick or as slow as I want. I enjoy my own company. I suppose I've got used to being alone for a long time. After a game I'm terrible. I can stay up until six in the morning and then go into training. I just watch videos or go for drives when there is nothing on the road – just driving and thinking.'

It promptly got worse. 'There's a lot of things I can't do,' he continued, 'like to have a dance with my girlfriend – I'd have to hire out a nightclub or something. That's the extent it's got to. It's stupid.' But there were compensations. 'It was love at first sight,' David went on. 'It's nice to have someone in your life you can talk to and spend time with.'

The time he did spend with Victoria was becoming, if anything, even more important to both of them. The two were now talking privately about marriage, as Victoria's mother Jackie inadvertently revealed. 'They're getting married, you know,' she said to a friend. 'Oh, I shouldn't have said anything.' Indeed not: this was not yet for public consumption. But after hastily changing the subject, Jackie revealed even more about the intense nature of David and Victoria's relationship, letting slip that while on tour Victoria slept in one of David's football shirts. 'She gets so lonely on these tours she sleeps in the shirt and it makes her feel closer to him,' she said.

Victoria herself was also becoming more forthcoming about her feelings for David. 'We buy each other presents and I love to buy my friends and family gifts because I can,' she said. 'I'm lucky that money isn't a worry now. And, of course, I love my clothes. That part of Posh Spice isn't an act. I do use my Gucci discount whenever I get the chance. But I'm not Posh Spice to David and he's not a famous soccer star to me. He understands the pressures and, like me, he'd rather cuddle up on the sofa watching *Blind Date* with a takeaway than be out at a club. David likes me for me. It's got nothing to do with the job I do. Most of the time we spend together we stay indoors and I wander around with no make-up and just a tracksuit on.'

The roller coaster continued. David flew to Paris to see Victoria but the flight developed problems, oxygen masks fell and the plane returned to Manchester. David simply waited for two hours and caught the next available plane. Victoria went on to Dusseldorf for the German première of *SpiceWorld: The Movie* and let slip more about their plans for the future. 'My boyfriend is a football player. We are soon getting married,' she was overheard to say, before adding, 'As soon as Gucci makes clothes for expectant mums, I would even consider a pregnancy.'

Victoria was then spotted visiting a bridal shop near her parents' home in Goff's Oak, Hertfordshire, and issued a furious denial that she was looking for a wedding dress. It then emerged that she was angry not about the wedding speculation but at the idea she would buy a wedding dress that was not by a world-famous designer.

Christmas approached and David and Victoria bought one another Rottweiler puppies named Snoop Doggy Dog and Puff Daddy, who lived mainly at David's house – 'They want something to cuddle when the other one isn't there,' said a friend.

The two then booked two suites, the Rolls and the Royce, at the Manchester Holiday Inn for the seasonal celebrations. One suite was to be used as a sitting room and the other for dinner: Victoria's parents attended but David's – perhaps tellingly, given that his father was later to complain David's fame kept them apart – did not. And the two gave each other presents just as lavish as would be expected: Victoria gave David an £11,000 gold and diamond bracelet, while he gave her a £13,000 jewel-studded cross. Victoria was nearly in tears when she showed it to friends.

The new year opened with a proposal. It was only 10 months since they had met but there was no doubt in either mind that the two were made for each other.

They had decided to get married when Victoria was on tour in the United States: now they could finally get around to making it official, and so met up at the five-star Rookery Hall Hotel in Nantwich, Cheshire, on 24 January 1998.

'While I was in America we decided we would get engaged,' Victoria said. 'I told him what my dream ring would be. He remembered and had it specially designed for me. We came here straight after the game and ordered champagne and dinner in our room. We were sitting there in our dressing gowns when David pulled out the ring, got down on one knee and said, "Will you marry me, Victoria?" I said yes, then produced my own ring and said, "Don't forget girl power – will you marry me?" I'd chosen the ring with my mum and dad in Los Angeles.' The happy couple plighted their troth, rang their parents – and then got in touch with their PR people.

It had been a momentous year for David, confirming him as one of the world's best up-and-coming footballers, as well as introducing him to the woman who was to become his wife. He and Victoria achieved what so many look for and so few find: they had become each other's other half. Two did become one in that union: they made each other complete. People who have spent time with the couple testify to the fact that when they are together – which is as often as they can conceivably manage – they are so intent upon one another that they almost seem in a world apart. And it should come as no surprise. Apart from a massive physical attraction, attested to by the fact they fancied one another before they actually met, the two have a great deal in common: fame, determination to succeed and the desire to put their children and each other before all else.

And this was just the beginning. As David and Victoria's relationship continued, they were to become greater than the sum of their two parts. They were to become icons, almost a brand in themselves, transcending David's prowess on the football pitch and Victoria's fame as a Spice Girl. They were to become Posh and Becks.

Chapter Five

Nothing Succeeds
Like Success

David's engagement to Victoria was not all he had
to celebrate at the beginning of 1998. His football
was going from good to marvellous, with United
beating Chelsea 5–3 just a couple of days into the
new year. Two of the goals were scored by David,
who then felt moved to give the Chelsea defender a
piece of his mind, calling him a 'little baby' after the
two of them had a near confrontation on the field.
United fans loved it and loved David. It seemed he
could do no wrong.

They loved Victoria, too – or at least some of them
did. In a hint of what was to come, Victoria's
relationship with her fiancé seemed to be arousing far
more interest than anything else the Spice Girls did
and, when the five girls went to film a special edition

of *Top Of The Pops*, Mel B encouraged the audience to ask anything they liked. Would Posh describe Becks, someone asked. Yes, she would. 'Let's just say he's the biggest and the best!' she chirped. 'Well, I only go for the best, naturally!'

And she was having an increasing influence on her man. David had always loved fashion – witness the comments from his teammates when he first joined United – but now he had someone to share that interest with. In January, he went to Milan to attend the Versace fashion show. 'David loves clothes and was thrilled at the invite,' said a friend. Whether his manager was so thrilled is debatable.

Now that the two were officially engaged, Victoria was also becoming increasingly open about their relationship and her feelings for David. 'I fell in love with David very quickly,' she said. 'I knew within a couple of weeks of that first kiss. I've had boyfriends before – I've been engaged before – but it never felt like it has with David. We just work so well together and being with him feels so right. I wanted to tell the world, but I had to hold back. I wanted to be sure he felt the same way. But he did. We were at my parents' again. David told me that he loved me and I said, "I love you too." And that was that.'

And what of the Spice Girls? Although, unbeknown to anyone, including the lady herself, Geri was to leave just a few months later, precipitating the break-up of the group, the girls were still hugely popular worldwide. Would the engagement cause any problems there? Apparently not. 'Getting married will not affect the future of the Spice Girls,' said Victoria. 'I sat them down a few weeks ago when we were in Australia to tell them that we were getting engaged and they were all thrilled. Like our song says, "If you wanna be my lover, you gotta get with my friends." David knows that the other girls are very, very important to me and I'm not sure I would have gone through with this if they didn't support me. Since then we've spent all our spare time talking about the wedding. They all want to be bridesmaids and there are already arguments about what shoes they're going to wear. I asked them not to wear those huge Buffalo trainers but they probably will.'

David was equally thrilled and equally unable to speak about anything else. 'Gary Neville will be my best man,' he confided. 'He's my best mate and was the man who first knew how I felt about Victoria. He'll already be getting nervous about his speech. The boss will be pleased. [sic] He doesn't interfere in our private lives. He just wants to make sure I keep myself fit and he trusts me. He met Victoria for the first time the other day. She asked him if he would be at their concert. He said, "Er, I don't know," and she started having a go, saying, "Well, I come to all your matches." He thought it was very funny – which was a relief.

'I wasn't at all nervous about getting engaged and we decided a while ago we would make it official this weekend. I got the ring and was really looking forward to it. But when the moment came there were a few butterflies. It was very funny when she pulled out a ring for me. Typical. I'm ready for all the wedding talk and plans. She's already started on about dresses and even the flowers. It'll be the best day of our lives.'

The rings in question were much discussed. Victoria's was a £40,000 solitaire diamond ring specially designed by Boodle & Dunthorne, while David's was a six-carat, diamond-encrusted band from a Los Angeles jeweller. 'It's lovely,' said Victoria, showing the ring off the next day. 'It's my dream ring. It's just what I wanted and it was a big surprise.' And how did she feel about being engaged? 'I'm all embarrassed now!' The publicity surrounding the rings, incidentally, caused another embarrassment for Victoria – customs took note and levied tax on the gift.

David was a true romantic. He arranged for Victoria to be given 30 roses when she arrived at the hotel and spent £200 filling their room with red and yellow roses and lilies. 'The colours and smell made it a perfect setting,' said a source at the hotel.

The two were not able to get married immediately – they knew it would be well over a year, taking busy schedules into account, before they were able to exchange their vows, but that did nothing to mar their happiness. 'They're so happy together,' said a spokesman for Victoria. 'They've had bottles of champagne sent up to their suite and are just thrilled to be spending some time with each other. Their parents are absolutely delighted.' Or to put it another way, Victoria's parents were. Tellingly, perhaps, David's father said he had only just heard the news and couldn't comment.

The engagement did nothing to quell the couple's passion for one another – quite the opposite in fact. Back on *Top Of The Pops*, the girls were asked when they last had sex in a public place. 'On a plane last night!' bellowed Mel B. The other girls were slightly more reticent – except Victoria. 'I'm not saying because my boyfriend wouldn't be happy … but it was recently and it was in my car!' she admitted. Girl power had never looked like so much fun.

As David's popularity grew, he began signing ever more lucrative sponsorship deals. The latest was a record seven-year, £4-million link-up with Adidas, prompting all sorts of criticism that David had become 'too big for his boots'. It was a charge he fiercely denied. 'A lot has been made about me supposedly getting too big for my boots,' he said plaintively. 'But the people who know me know that isn't true. A lot of things have changed in my life – but the way I am hasn't. I have a lot of people who will knock me down if I do change. Alex Ferguson hasn't said, "Cut it out," because he doesn't think I'm doing anything wrong. He has told me I'm handling everything well. Glenn Hoddle doesn't see a problem, either. And the other players don't.'

At the time, certainly, Ferguson was showing his support. A hamstring injury forced David to be left out of a friendly – England v Chile – but Ferguson talked only of his concern about David and the team. There was, however, another jarring note when it emerged that Victoria was not happy about living up north, with rumours that she was holding Beckham back from buying a house.

And the downside of fame was beginning to emerge. A gang of thugs stole David's car and set it on fire. He had a stalker, a man who followed him always wearing a crash helmet to disguise his face. And then, to cap it all, bullets were sent through the post, with David's name engraved on them. Naturally, he informed the police and increased the amount of security at his £200,000 home in Worsley, Salford. 'This has really upset David,' said a friend. 'He is busy turning his home into a fortress. He was really upset when the bullets came through the post – especially when he saw they had his name carved on them.'

Poor David. He was heard to ask, 'Why pick on me? What have I done to them?' Nothing, of course – but by now David was worth an estimated £10 million, was earning £20,000 a week, was very good-looking, drove flash cars and was engaged to one of the most famous women on the planet. We live in a society that is obsessed with celebrity – and the downside for celebrities is when jealousy begins to take hold.

It might have been the stress, but David's temper

boiled up in a match against Chelsea, with the result that he was given the yellow card. This was serious, not least because the World Cup was approaching and David was on the England team. The then England manager Glenn Hoddle expressed his concern, saying that he would have to have a meeting with David to tell him to calm down. 'David got booked again needlessly and we will have to talk,' he said. 'He had a similar problem for us in Le Tournoi last year and we can't afford that sort of behaviour at the World Cup finals this summer.' It was an ominous warning of what was to come.

And this World Cup was attracting a good deal of attention. There was intense speculation as to whether Paul Gascoigne, once the wonder boy of football and increasingly more famous for his drinking bouts, would be included in the team. Meanwhile, David's soaring public profile was continuing to cause concern. He was pictured having dinner with Victoria in Paris, in the middle of the Spice Girls' world tour, causing a whole nation of sports writers to pour their hearts out, imploring him not to neglect the beautiful game.

And by now David really was just a step away from the status of national treasure – a status he himself managed to postpone during the forthcoming World Cup – but seemed, at least, to retain his modesty. Asked how he coped with his fame, David replied, 'The other day I was round at Victoria's house and the postman rang the bell to deliver something. I went and answered the door and his jaw dropped. "Blimey," he said, "I never thought I'd see a legend this early in the morning." But that's just daft. I'm only 22. I haven't done anything.' Clearly, Beckham's feet – when they weren't making music on the football pitch – were still firmly on the ground.

But his superstar status meant that very few others saw him in such a modest light. In April the Spice Girls held a press conference at the Nymex Arena: David went along to see Victoria and attracted such a crush of people that he had to retire backstage.

Meanwhile, at the same event, Victoria revealed a baby was on the cards. 'I'm practising to get pregnant!' she informed the 150 enthralled reporters present. 'Victoria, it's outrageous!' said Mel B. 'You are not even married!'

Beckham had still not calmed down on the field, though. He continued to lose his temper easily, prompting concerns that he could follow in the increasingly troubled path of Paul Gascoigne. In retrospect, that was clearly never going to happen. Unlike Gascoigne, David was a model of restraint off the pitch – it was only when he was actually playing that he sometimes lost control. He also had a clear-headedness about his career that stood him in good stead, revealing in an interview that he had been terrified of failing to make the grade.

'The first time I really got into the squad the manager wasn't using me a lot,' he said. 'I was on the bench and sometimes I wasn't even getting changed. That kept me hungry. I always wanted to be there. And, once I got a taste for it, I felt sort of embarrassed if I wasn't there. When I got to Manchester, I didn't want people down in London saying, "Oh, he'll be back in a couple of years because he's crap." And I was worried they would also be saying that I hadn't made the standard. It was sort of an embarrassment.'

By this time it was more than clear that David had made the standard, but it was clearly still a cause for anxiety – and that was probably to be welcomed. Once stars in any field start to believe their own publicity, they are almost certainly lost – and that was not a trap David was falling into. Snooker champion Ronnie O'Sullivan, a friend of Beckham's, revealed that David helped him to cope with the downside of fame.

'It can all get too much sometimes,' he said. 'But I've got people to share the problems with – as well as the good times – and that helps. I remember meeting David Beckham in a club near where we are both from, in Chingford, three years ago. It was before he was famous. We hit it off and he would invite me up to Manchester for games of pool. The only problem was he'd beat me – he's a right hustler. I called him just before United's semi-final against Borussia Dortmund last year and I wished him all the best. People might want to be a snooker player like me, but I want to be a footballer like David. I love watching him because he is so dangerous. He does things on the field that make you sit up and take notice, like I try to do on the snooker table.'

And David's innate modesty showed no signs of disappearing. He professed himself unmoved by Victoria's star status, saying, 'I like Victoria for herself, not anything else. I'd like her if she worked in Tesco. We both understand the pressures of fame and encourage each other to ignore it or we laugh about it. She's more famous than me anyway! Some days I find four or five girls crying outside the door. I can't understand how people get like that.' And his teammates also helped to keep his head from swelling. After he got engaged, 'I got a lot of flak from the lads,' he said. 'I walked in and they started whistling "Here Comes The Bride".'

The couple were charming everyone. On a shopping trip to Harrods, David parked his Porsche on a yellow line: the traffic warden took one look at the car's passengers and let them off the £60 fine. In return he was rewarded with two autographs. And finally, after months of speculation as to where they would live, David and Victoria bought a £300,000 penthouse flat in the exclusive village of Alderley Edge in Cheshire. Their first purchase for their new property was a £40,000 kitchen from Harrods.

As the World Cup drew ever nearer, David did not let up. In May his autobiography, *My Story*, was published, revealing, if nothing else, his growing love of modelling. The book was filled with pictures of the star. 'I can't actually believe I've brought a book out!' he said, before defending himself once more against the charge of arrogance. 'I'm not the person a lot of people think I am,' he said. 'A lot of people think I'm dead flash and dead arrogant, which I'm not.'

He also revealed that the best revenge against the naysayers was, well, success. For some time now rival supporters had taken to singing an obscene song about Victoria's sexual preferences: how did he cope? 'It's pretty difficult when you're young and you're getting that sort of stick off crowds,' he said. 'It's hard to get used to. It's not as if they're saying it about your football: they're saying it about your private life. But, every time they've said it, I've gone and scored.' (Victoria, incidentally, who has a much better sense of humour than she is usually credited with, laughed it off, once telling a story about a partly deaf old lady who said how nice it was that the fans were singing about her).

However, David still seemed bemused by his fame. 'It's a shame that my new hairstyle can make the front of the papers when there's so many more important things going on in the world,' he said. 'It shocks me. There's kids all over the world that are losing lives and losing families and then because I've gone blond it's on the front of the paper. It's not my fault. When I go to a restaurant, it's not because I want to go and get my picture taken, it's because I want to go and have a nice meal. I can't go to a nice restaurant in a tracksuit. I have to dress up for my picture.'

And of his relationship with Sir Alex, David was fulsome, in his own unique way. 'He frightens the hell out of players, but when you have a manager for so many years, you get used to his ways,' he said. 'The best thing is, you know where you stand. If you've done terrible in a game, he'll tell you straight down the line and the next day he'll forget about it. He doesn't hold grudges. He's the best manager I've ever had. Well, he's the only manager I've had at this level. But he's the best manager I've ever had.'

David also remembered his month with Preston – a month that was clearly proving to be invaluable as his fame grew, not least because it made him appreciate how lucky he was. 'Usually, you walk into United and your kit's laid out, nice brand new towel, nice clean everything – underwear, shorts, the lot,' he said. 'I turned up there and there was nothing. They had to give me odds and sods from all over the place.' In addition, unlike at United, David was expected to wash his own kit.

The World Cup was now weeks away and David nipped to France for a quick holiday with Victoria. He was now concerned both about the upcoming event and his next season with United – the team had failed to win any honours this season. 'We can't expect to win the Championship every season,' said David diplomatically. 'Teams are trying that bit harder to beat us. But we will be even more determined in the

Premiership and the Champions League next season. We're a team of winners. Most of the lads have known only success, so second place is not good enough. The last two years in Europe we have been so near and yet so far. It's time to make it third time lucky.'

And now the big one was looming – and David was still attracting attention for his dress sense. In June, weeks before the start of the World Cup, it emerged that he wore a new pair of Adidas Predator boots every time he played for England. Retailing at £200 a throw and specially designed with the word 'Becks' on the heel, David by now had seven pairs – but said that he could not play as well in them after they had been worn once.

But a far bigger fuss blew up when David flew off for another short break with Victoria in the South of France, where the two stayed at Sir Elton John's £3.5-million pink mansion on the Côte d'Azur. The two went out for a romantic dinner at the Chèvre D'Or restaurant in Eze sur Mer and dressed for the occasion: Victoria wore trousers and David wore a sarong. It was a Louisiana print silk square by Jean Paul Gaultier costing £115 and it was worn over a pair of loose linen trousers, but David could scarcely have commanded more attention if he had said he was flying to the moon. Sarongs promptly sold out at London's Gallery Gaultier, while the great and the good, both of football and fashion, queued up to give their point of view.

Alan Hansen, the former Liverpool defender turned BBC commentator, turned up at, appropriately enough, the launch of the Menswear Council and defended Beckham's look. 'At Liverpool, other players used to laugh at John Barnes for wearing his fancy suits,' he said. 'You would hear a groan go around the tour bus the minute he arrived each morning, but I thought he looked great.'

Also present was Chris Scott-Gray, director of the Menswear Council. 'It's great to see a footballer in something other than muddy kit or a flashy suit that doesn't suit him,' he said. 'Beckham can get away with the sarong because he is young, but clothes and style are not necessarily a youth thing. British men have never seemed to master the straightforward rules of dressing. They seem to give up once they've passed their 20s – when they dress to pull.' David was not concerned. By now even he had begun to realise that if he wore something unusual it would be commented on – and it was.

Worse – far worse – was to come. The Spice Girls, now minus Geri, gave an interview to *Smash Hits* magazine and, among all the bewilderment at Halliwell's departure, someone thought to ask Victoria about Beckham's sarong. 'It's nothing out of the ordinary,' Victoria said brightly. 'David wears my knickers as well. He's getting in touch with his feminine side.'

This light-hearted joke was one day to plague David, to the extent that he had to deny it on national television. But this time round, no one noticed. Victoria has a very sharp sense of humour and clearly thought everyone she was talking to would realise it was a joke as well. And the fact that no one made a fuss about it finally led Victoria to tell it again – at which point everyone did notice and the resulting furore went on for months. But that particular episode lay ahead.

It is testimony to David's steadiness of character that he had no problem with Victoria claiming he wore women's underwear. He has always been a mature young man and, because of his modesty, shyness and high-pitched voice, it is often easy to forget quite what an extraordinary young man he is. But this incident, trivial as it was, illustrates quite how different David is from the vast majority of players of the beautiful game. He doesn't mind being called feminine, he flaunts his love of clothing and jewellery – and he doesn't even mind being called a gay icon. Other footballers would have quit the game (or at least beaten their tormentors to a pulp) for less – and David barely noticed what was going on.

As the onset of the World Cup approached, David attracted more attention than ever. His wealth was beginning to become a serious issue, by this time estimated at nearly £10 million. This was made up of a £1.35 million salary with Man U plus a further £8 million in sponsorship fees. Every time he changed his hairstyle he made the front pages. He wanted women to become involved in the macho world of football. He didn't mind having Victoria cited as the one who wore the trousers in the relationship – unless it upset her. But David's mind was now on higher things – the World Cup.

Initially, all seemed to be well. There had been a huge uproar when it emerged that Paul Gascoigne was not, after all, to play with the team, but this had largely died down as attention shifted to the players who would actually be there. The focus was on David's teammate, Teddy Sheringham, who had attracted some flak when he was caught out drinking in the Algarve. David was supportive.

'It is not my place to make any sort of judgement on Teddy – that is down to the England boss,' he said. 'But what I will say is that, knowing Teddy as I do, I have no doubt he will be up for it at the World Cup. No way, whatever has happened, whatever has been going on, will he not be totally fit and ready. I'm sure the events of the last few days will give him an even greater incentive to prove everyone wrong.'

They were fine words, loyal and supportive of a colleague, although not everyone was entirely happy. Then, quite suddenly, the focus shifted and David found that it was he, now, who was the centre of attention – when the England manager Glenn Hoddle dropped him from England's opening match against Tunisia, replacing him with Darren Anderton. David was devastated, as were his fans – and, ironically given later events, Alex Ferguson.

Sir Bobby Charlton, himself a former World Cup

winner, spoke out. 'Alex Ferguson has already said that he was a little disappointed that Glenn Hoddle put David Beckham in front of his press corps and I would have to agree with that,' he said. 'David wants to be the best player in the world. He just knows he has so much skill and ability and I don't think he understands why he's not playing. He has an ability which isn't anywhere else in the team. His passing and ability to score goals, the quality of his crossing if he plays on the right side. You're looking at one of the rare players in the world. He's got fantastic ability.'

It was now Teddy Sheringham's turn to speak out for his friend. 'Yes, David is very down,' he said. 'I was surprised he wasn't chosen, especially as he played in all the eight qualifiers – perhaps it's a sign of all the excellent players we have now.'

Hoddle himself was defiant. 'We won 2–0. I don't have to justify my selections,' he snapped.

Beckham was becoming increasingly distressed about the situation, although he was doing his best to be dignified. 'I have had a few days to think about it and I still don't know what went wrong,' he said. 'The manager did sit down and explain a few things, but it was more a pat on the back. I did ask him why I wasn't there but I'd rather keep the answer between us. He just sees some things different to me.'

But the strain was beginning to tell – not least because of the unvoiced suspicion that Beckham was being punished for getting too big for his boots again.

Asked by one journalist if he hadn't been chosen because he had a difficult personality, David finally snapped. 'There's people who don't know me as a person and they shouldn't start judging me,' he said furiously. 'I don't think I have done anything wrong in terms of what happens around me. Stuff goes on because people take pictures of me and want pictures of me when I'm out. Just because I've got a famous girlfriend doesn't mean I'm up in the clouds and no one can speak to me. I didn't sulk, like a few people suggested. I didn't say much to the manager. I asked questions and he gave answers but he did not say I wouldn't be playing again, thank goodness.

'You could argue I wasn't reproducing my usual form and I have heard it said that I dipped. Maybe in a couple of games I was tired but the manager picked me in every one that mattered and I don't think my form has been affected that much. It would have been nice just to play for 10 minutes against Tunisia and I think I would have felt better, had I got on. But the manager has his team and he sticks with that. In the end there's nothing I can do or say if that's his decision.'

Poor David. It was an uncharacteristic outburst and indicative of an anger building up inside him that was to have catastrophic consequences.

Hoddle was livid – not just with David, but with Ferguson. 'David was not focused coming in to the tournament – he was vague – and maybe his club need to look at that further,' he snapped. 'I had a chat with him and he's more focused now but I needed to have words before that sunk in. I love him to bits. After all, I brought him in. But he's got to understand that football comes first. His focus was not there, but now he understands what I'm looking for.'

Ironically, given that Sir Alex came to share those views and might already have been feeling them himself, Hoddle now rounded on the Man U manager. 'Everyone is different, but I would never put that sort of pressure on Alex Ferguson before a big European game,' he said, referring to Ferguson's comments about Beckham. 'To come out with some of the things he said on the eve of a World Cup game was unprofessional. People can have their own opinions and they are welcome to them. It's a bit disappointing, but it's not just Ferguson doing it – there are other people, on TV and in newspapers.'

There were indeed. Calls were growing for David to be brought on and he finally was – he came on as a substitute for the second match with Romania. 'The disappointment has lifted suddenly,' said a beaming Beckham. Matters improved yet further: David scored a goal in England's next match against Colombia, leading to a 2–0 win. It was a 30-yard free kick – and it brought the house (or rather, the stadium) down. Hoddle maintained that it had come about by keeping David back, but no one really cared any more. Beckham was back, he was scoring brilliant goals and

it seemed that absolutely nothing could go wrong.
David himself was more excited than ever and was
busy preparing for what he hoped would be the game
of the season: England versus Argentina.

Top: One of the world's greatest footballers as a child with his mum and dad already proud of his up-and-coming skills.

Bottom left: A young David Beckham collecting an award at Old Trafford in 1986. Bobby Charlton stands over him.

Bottom right: Within the boy's frame – a remarkably mature determination to succeed.

Top left: Becks keeping up on the sports pages whilst in Spain on a trip he won to the Barcelona F.C. youth academy with the Bobby Charlton Soccer School. To his left is Stuart Leigh.

Top right: On the same trip to Barcelona, with Terry Venables.

Bottom: A very little David is the first on the left in the front row. His father stands, in blue, clapping on the back row.

Top: David Beckham joins Manchester United on the day of his 14th birthday. His family and Alex Ferguson stand in the background.

Bottom: Young but already powerful – Beckham in flight.

Top left: David with Eric Cantona. During this time, David was lodging with Annie and Tommy Kay in Manchester.

Top right: The Kay's house where David lived between the ages of 16 and 21.

Bottom: Beckham making his league debut for Manchester United against Leeds United.

David Beckham's was a swift rise – here he is seen carrying the 1997 P.F.A. Young Player of the Year cup.

There's only one David Beckham! David celebrates scoring for England in the 1998 World Cup against Colombia.

Top: The man in action. Yet another Beckham goal, this time against Chelsea.

Bottom left: The perfect gentleman off the pitch, David's passionate relationship with football has sometimes got him in trouble whilst on the grass. Here he vents his frustration at referee Gerald Ashby during a match against Leicester City.

Bottom right: Four great footballers: (*From left*) Ryan Giggs, Denis Irwin, Teddy Sheringham, David Beckham and Andy Cole all in the famous Man U red.

The post-match meeting in Old Trafford that was to lead to one of the most-publicised romances of our time.

Chapter Six

From Hero to Zero

It was, said the papers, a 'moment of madness'. For England fans, it was the end of a dream and one man was responsible – David Beckham. The act itself was over in a trifle, but it lost England the match and the title. David Beckham was fouled by the Argentine skipper Diego Simeone and, in a display of petulance, tripped him up. Simeone appeared to collapse in agony, David was promptly sent off and, with only 10 men now in the team, it was all but impossible to win. After Beckham's departure, the team staged an extraordinary resistance to Argentina, forcing the match into extra time and then to a penalty shootout, but it was no good. They drew 2–2, but Argentina won 4–3 on penalties.

Until Beckham's departure shortly after half-time, England had a real chance of winning the match. The teenage player Michael Owen had scored a goal and his euphoria had rubbed off on his teammates. But, after Beckham's idiocy, the mood changed dramatically – and Glenn Hoddle appeared utterly vindicated in his decision to hold Beckham back for so long, fearing just such an outburst. 'That cost us dearly,' said a sombre Hoddle after the match. 'With 10 men, we defended like lions. It's a bitter, bitter pill to take and we are absolutely distraught but proud at the same time. I don't know if it was destiny, everything just went against us. It's not a night for excuses, it's a night for us to be proud for England.'

The backlash was immediate – and huge. Beckham had been warned over and over again about losing his temper on the field and, although Diego Simeone was clearly quite as guilty as David, it did not excuse Beckham's action. He, himself, immediately realised what he had done and England's footballing great and good were quick off the mark to absolve him – perhaps realising quite how hostile the public reaction was going to be.

First off the bench was Sir Bobby Charlton. 'You cannot throw him to the wolves,' he said. 'I saw him after the match and he was terribly affected by it. He realised what he had done. I have not seen any replays but David Beckham was brought down and reacted by kicking out, for which he was given a red card. That came after England's great first-half performance and it was always going to be difficult against one of the best sides in the world.

'Everyone knows the consequences of reacting. He's a young lad and he's paid a very high price. He is a young man who was very much affected by it, I know that, and he will have other World Cups where he can put that right. But it made life difficult for the rest of his team and he appreciates this, too.'

Next up, unsurprisingly, was Victoria. She was on tour in the States with the Spice Girls and had watched the match live in New York. She, also, was only too aware of what lay in store for her fiancé. 'Please don't hate him,' she implored. 'He doesn't deserve to be the most hated man in Britain. He, more than anyone, wanted England to go all the way. I am as upset as everyone in Britain. David needs my support. I just want to be with him. We love each other very much and it is important to get us through this.'

Indeed, the only person David wanted to see was Victoria. He left France with the rest of the team to return home by Concorde, wincing visibly at the sight of the massed photographers. He then flew straight to New York, where the two were reunited. But, before going, clearly devastated by the turn of events, David issued a public apology to the country. 'This is, without doubt, the worst moment of my career and I will always regret what I did,' he said. 'I have apologised to my England teammates and manager

Glenn Hoddle and I want every English supporter to know how sorry I am.'

He clearly was, but matters rapidly got worse. Adidas pulled two television commercials starring the beleaguered player, saying they had 'run their course. They were only scheduled to run as long as England were in the tournament. It is pointless having ads on British television while England are no longer playing.' David was fined £2,000 for his conduct (admittedly, it wouldn't have made that much of a dent in his wallet) and, much worse, banned from the next two England games, thus missing out on the opening stages of the next European Championship qualifying campaign.

Manchester United, however closed ranks around their young player. 'Beckham was playing in an international match so we don't think it would be appropriate to say anything at club level,' said a spokesman.

But the real problem for Beckham was growing anger among the fans, so much so that even Glenn Hoddle, who had earlier asserted that England could have won had they been playing with 11 men, stepped in to defend David. 'I hope that fans are going to be fair,' he said. 'He's reacted in a foolish way and has to understand that he can't react like that again. Why do we always need a scapegoat? He put in a fantastic performance against Colombia, but all that gets forgotten.

'David's had to take a bit of stick already in his

career and it will be sad if that gets worse because of this, but that's the nature of our game. I would plead with people to look at the positive aspect of his games in an England shirt, although he's a strong enough character to take it on the chin. David is very down but we will have a chat and he's got to learn from it. We must not go overboard about it – it's not a time to blame anybody.

'What David did wasn't violent conduct and it shouldn't have been a red card. Then again, it was such a foolish thing to do and he has to understand that he can't do those sorts of things at this level. We've been trying to drum that into him for some time but there's no blame to be put on anybody's shoulders here. He might even become a better player if he goes on to learn from this.'

Support even came from Italy. Inter Milan goalkeeper Gianluca Pagliuca made clear his disgust at his teammate's behaviour as the team warmed up to face Holland. Referring to the way Simeone appeared to roll around the ground clutching his leg in agony, Pagliuca snorted, 'I know Simeone well and he was playacting.'

But none of this was enough to save Beckham from the wrath of the fans. And even Glenn Hoddle, despite his earlier calming statement, issued a thinly veiled threat to drop David from the England team unless he cleaned up his act – and fast. 'Will what happened influence my selection of David?' he asked.

'It depends on what I see from now until our next game. Even if I still think what he did really only warranted a yellow card, the fact is the players have got to deal with the rules as they stand and he did a stupid thing. He has to learn from what happened. He needs to deal with it, his club needs to deal with it and I need to deal with it.' David was clearly a long way from being forgiven.

And indeed, the first indications about what the England fans thought of him were coming to light. United's first away game was to be against West Ham in August: supporters hung a threatening poster at the gates of Upton Park, the club's ground, a full six weeks before the match. Sir Alex Ferguson leaped to his player's defence. 'We will be looking after the player and we will protect him, because that is the way Manchester United behave,' he said. 'We are a great club and we will not be giving in to mob rule. I admit there are sound reasons for thinking it would make sense for David to go and play abroad, but that would be the easy way out. In any case, he doesn't want to leave Old Trafford. He's Manchester United through and through.'

But the fans were not appeased. An editorial appeared on the website Football365, a daily soccer paper, under the headline, 'It Is Our Duty To Taunt Him'. It pulled no punches. 'It is our patriotic duty to give him hell verbally next season,' it read. 'Relentlessly. We need to demonstrate some imagination. There is no point in just booing him all the time. He will soon get used to it. So sometimes we need a slow handclap. On other occasions, whistles or deadly silence – not a murmur from the crowd when he's in possession. When he can cope with all this and not run whinging to his agent or manager or Italy, then we will know he is up to wearing the Three Lions once more.' The editor of the site insisted the piece was tongue-in-cheek.

Could it get worse? Oh yes. In fact, the persecution of Beckham had hardly begun. Pub owner Phil Murray made it personal when he sued David over loss of earnings, arguing that, after England dropped out of the World Cup, his pub, the Horse and Groom at Islingwood, East Sussex, suffered a loss in takings. 'We were packed when England played,' he said. 'Trade went up 200 per cent and the atmosphere was brilliant. But I've never seen a pub empty as fast after we finally lost. Beckham should realise his silly kick ruined England's chances and cost the licensed trade millions.'

Beckham was fast realising a great deal. His parents, Ted and Sandra, were becoming targets themselves: thugs were abusing them on their doorstep, sending hate mail and damaging the house. The pair were guarded until the furore wore down. Even worse, an effigy of David was hung outside the Pleasant Pheasant pub in South Norwood, London, until the police ordered it to be taken down.

Ted Beckham was distraught. 'He's made one

mistake and been absolutely slaughtered for it,' he said. 'All he wants to do is play football. He'll go back to training but, after that, I don't know. It's too early to say whether he'll stay in England or go abroad. It's what David decides. But whatever he does, I'll support him. I spoke to David on Sunday night and he's very low – he hardly mentioned football.

'He's feeling very low. He knows he has got to come back and face up to it some time – and he's got training to think of. But he's very apprehensive. I'm no longer proud to be British after what they've done to my son – all for a game of football. He's made a mistake. We all know he's made a mistake but he's certainly paying for it now. I'm disgusted with what has gone on. I've had enough. I'm just glad David's been out of the country. He hasn't seen half of what's gone on and I won't let him.'

David did finally return in mid-July, looking absolutely wretched. His old teammate Gary Pallister spoke out in support. 'I don't think David will want to run away,' he said. 'He is a strong enough character to face the music and face the pressure. Knowing David as I do and knowing the club as I do, David will get all the support he needs. The manager and his assistant Brian Kidd will look after him and will have had a talk with him. They will have talked it through and will have put his mind at rest. I am sure Becks is used to the flak from away supporters because of his personal life and the fact that he has been successful at a young age and he has been able to handle it. He got a lot of stick last season because of his private life. He has already had schooling in dealing with away fans, who use him as a target. I really don't see what more supporters can do.'

It was a miserable time. David went around dressed all in black, with a black hat covering his hair, clearly trying to look as inconspicuous as possible. His misery was so apparent that the golfer Lee Westwood called for him to be left alone. 'It's sad when the public can't look upon sport as a game,' he said. 'At the end of the day, it is not life and death. David got sent off against Argentina and probably regrets it, but what can he do about it? When tensions are high and there's a lot of passion, you do things and sometimes you say things you don't mean. I think it is sad. Football, like golf, is just a game. You can go home and do whatever you want and forget about it and no one is hurt, are they? It's not like a war, although some people treat it like that, which is the wrong attitude.'

Even George Michael came to his support, comparing David's ordeal to his own public disgrace when he was arrested in a Beverly Hills public lavatory. 'Even though I was as pissed off with him as we all were, let's be honest, one little mistake ... well, I can relate, man.'

Training began in mid-July and, for the first time in over a month, David began to look a little bit more cheerful. He was caught horsing around on the field with Teddy Sheringham: the latter pushed Beckham off the ball and David responded by flicking his right foot at him as a joke. He even managed a smile. Everyone began to relax a little and David even began to be able to walk around the streets near his home again without causing a riot.

The locals were supportive. 'I think people are rallying right behind him and are more than a little bit appalled at the abuse he has been getting,' said Kevin Meredith, who owned the local newsagent's. 'David normally comes in here every morning for his newspapers but the last couple of days he has stayed in the car while his father has fetched them.'

Even the West Ham supporters, who had been threatening David with a terrible reception, began to calm down. Shane Barber, who edits a West Ham fanzine, had been about to launch a 10,000-red-card campaign against poor Beckham, in which 10,000 supporters would wave red cards at the fallen hero, but it was called off shortly before the match. 'It won't go ahead – it's got out of hand.'

Even so, it was at this time that a move to Real Madrid was first suggested. Such was the intensity of the feelings aroused that many believed David would simply not be able to continue living in this country. But the fact was that David didn't want to go – and neither, back then, did Sir Alex Ferguson wish to lose his brilliant player. David was not, however, quite up to facing the public yet: he pulled out of a friendly against Birmingham. His England teammate Gareth

Southgate, who had himself been the recipient of venom from the fans when he missed in a penalty shootout against Germany in the semi-final of Euro '96, warned David that he would just have to take it.

'The next few weeks are not going to be very nice for David,' he said. 'The poor lad has already gone through far more than I ever suffered, but I can still give him some good advice because of my own experience. I took a lot of stick, including verbal abuse, nasty letters and people crossing the road to avoid me. The way you deal with it is the important thing and I was determined to stand up, be a man and try to explain to all those critics that football is merely a game.

'Eventually, the tide turned for me. Most people were sympathetic and I am certain this will be the case for David as well. I have every confidence he can win this battle, even though it is going to be hard for him – very, very hard. David seems a quiet lad, yet I have no doubt he possesses the character and personality to come out the other side. He wouldn't have progressed as far as he has in the game without a lot of inner strength. None of the England players blame David. We should never have been forced to take on Argentina in the second round, because other things could have been done by the management to avoid that fixture. David has been made a scapegoat. The public have reacted entirely wrongly. Incidents such as his effigy being hung from a lamp-post are utterly disgusting.'

David must have been enormously heartened by those words and even more so when he played in a friendly in Oslo against part-timers Valerenga. It was his first game since the match against Argentina and he was given a hero's welcome, with 20,000 fans roaring their approval as the teams were read out. Even before the match began, the fans were determined to tell David he was out of the wilderness: he was presented with a Player of the Year trophy by the Norwegian branch of the United fan club.

It was the perfect setting for David to make his first appearance and it showed. For the first time the haunted look he had been wearing for the past seven weeks began to slip and his joy in acknowledging the fans spoke for itself. The only fly in the ointment was that he sprained his ankle and so was forced to miss out a friendly a couple of days later with Danish side Brondby – but, given his new status as the returned prodigal son, it was a small price to pay.

A sure sign that David was being forgiven came when people began to joke about what he had done. An Internet site posted a game in which players scored if they made a virtual David foul rival players – and scored even more if they managed to do so as a cartoon figure of Victoria flashed her knickers. It was childish – and exactly what the country needed to put recent events into perspective.

There were still rumblings from some quarters, not least when United played Arsenal at Wembley and rival fans gave David to understand that they had not been pleased with his actions, but they were increasingly muted. United itself could not have been more supportive, not least when, in mid-August, David signed a new five-year £6 million contract with the club. Fears that he might leave the country had been proved wrong. 'I'm delighted to commit myself to the club long-term,' he said. 'This is where I grew up and where I want to stay. It's a great start to the new season for me because it's a special club with some very special players.'

Alex Ferguson also expressed his delight. 'I am really pleased,' he said. 'This obviously confirms United's intentions to have all of their major players signed on long-term deals. It speaks very highly of our players' commitment to the club and United's commitment to them and their futures.'

The shows of support were becoming increasingly public as David worked – or rather, played – his way back into the nation's heart. United played Leicester at Old Trafford, resulting in a 2–2 draw, with David scoring one of the goals. Some members of the crowd had been booing but the majority were in support, something acknowledged by David as he raised his right fist in tribute. He was publicly embraced on the field both by United's assistant manager Brian Kidd and by Leicester's Robbie Savage, a friend of David's and someone who had played with him in United's Youth team. Savage did, however, warn that it was not over yet. 'I'm afraid this is going to go on for months,' he said. 'David has to go to West Ham next week, when it will be different again. And I suspect that, when United come to Leicester, he'll still be getting some stick.'

Indeed, that West Ham match was seen as something of a potential crisis point for the player – it was, after all, West Ham fans who had been planning the red-card protest. But then, a couple of things happened to divert everyone's attention – and they both, needless to say, involved Victoria. The Spice Girls were still on tour in the United States, where they posed for a sensational photo shoot for the gay magazine *Attitude*, dressing up as members of the camp 1970s band Village People. In the accompanying interview Victoria revealed quite how famous she and David had become as a couple, when she recounted a meeting with Madonna at which David was present. 'She was acting like she knew us,' said a slightly overawed Posh. 'I said, "This is my boyfriend," and she said, "Yes. You're the footballer." He was saying, "I can't believe Madonna knows who I am."'

But far, far more significant than that was the revelation that Victoria was three months pregnant. That time in the South of France had clearly proved fruitful and David and Victoria, both of whom were keen to start a family, were thrilled. 'I'm absolutely delighted,' said Victoria, speaking publicly for the first time about the baby. 'The baby wasn't planned but I never for one moment considered not keeping it. Why would I? I love David, we are getting married and would have had children fairly soon anyway. I kept the pregnancy quiet just in case something went wrong. But I'm over three months now and I don't mind everyone knowing how happy I am.'

After all the drama of the summer, there could have been nothing better to cheer up David again – and to take his mind off that forthcoming match.

Indeed, Victoria related quite how overwhelmed David had been when she revealed the good news. 'When I told David I was pregnant, he just started weeping,' she said. 'He must have cried for about an hour and I had tears running down my face, too. It was a very emotional moment for both of us. The baby wasn't planned so it was a surprise mixed with real delight. I think telling David he was going to be a dad really put things in perspective for him because I know he's had such a hard year professionally.'

As if one Spice pregnancy wasn't enough, Mel B then revealed that she, too, was pregnant by the dancer Jimmy Gulzar, and was going to step up the aisle with him before the baby was born. It was very nearly a case of dancing in the streets – except at the girls' record company, that is, where bosses were said not to be holding celebrations about the news.

David, however, was still saying nothing publicly. That dreaded West Ham match was finally upon him and a mob of about 500 fans behaved appallingly, signalling that they, at least, had not forgiven him. David was pelted with stones and hit with a beer glass as the crowd booed and jeered him, and his good news. And their fury was not solely because of the World Cup: many were enraged that a player from east London should be part of the United team. David behaved magnificently: he rose above it all, said nothing and got on with the game, which resulted in a 0–0 draw. The crowd finally fell silent and David was able to leave the match with his dignity – and all his bones – intact.

That match really did signal an end to the hostilities. David had clearly suffered badly through anguish and remorse; he had endured a display of vitriolic hatred quite out of proportion to anything he had done – and now, as a father-to-be, he was ready to move on.

Victoria finally returned to England in September and, with David, made her first public appearance – fittingly enough – at the christening of her sister Louise's daughter Liberty. All the Spice Girls were clearly revelling in the situation. Mel B told Radio 1 that she and Victoria 'turned into dragons. It was kinda funny'. Meanwhile, Victoria said of her pregnancy, 'It's something we all look forward to. It's only natural. We've all said having a family was something we wanted.'

Being back in England did have a downside, though. So much had happened since Victoria had gone away – David's red card and its aftermath, and her pregnancy – that photographers were even more desperate than usual to capture pictures of the couple. This led to a nasty incident at a service station on the motorway. Victoria and the girls had been playing at a concert in Sheffield, after which she and David were driven back to his home in Cheshire in a chauffeured Mercedes. Once on the M62 they noticed a car following them, and so the car sped up before pulling up at a service station. Their pursuer, a photographer, tried to take pictures of Victoria, who was apparently wearing a dressing gown, at which point David got into a fight with the man and the police were called.

'It was beyond belief. It really was a devilish experience,' a tearful Victoria said later. 'We accept we will be photographed but there is a lot of difference between that and pursuing someone like you are on a foxhunt. The whole incident left me shaken and very upset. I truly feared for my unborn baby.'

The police were extremely sympathetic. 'It was quite frightening for Victoria, especially as she is expecting a baby,' said a spokesman. 'They were chased for some time and when they pulled up to get some petrol he tried to take a picture of Victoria. She had got changed and was trying to relax. She was wearing her dressing gown. David was very angry and they had an argument. The police were called. It did get quite serious. Both parties were spoken to and no further action will be taken.'

As the couple revelled in being together again, David continued to redeem himself on the field. Playing against Barcelona in late September, David delivered one of his wonder goals, which drew praise not only from Glenn Hoddle but even Barcelona's goalkeeper, the Dutch Ruud Hesp. 'I knew where it was going once he struck it, but he has such a brilliant ability in these situations that there was no easy way to get to the ball,' he said. 'If he catches it right, I doubt there is any goalkeeper in the world who can stop him. People might say, if you know where it's going why doesn't the keeper move further over? But, if you go too far, he'd spot that and hit it into the opposite corner.'

It was not only business as usual as far as football was concerned: David's interest in fashion had flared up again, too. He and Victoria attended Antonio Berardi's catwalk show during London Fashion Week and were mobbed by an enthusiastic crowd shortly afterwards.

But yet more drama was in store. It was not only rogue photographers who were out to cause trouble; 'glamour models' were out to do their bit, too. And so it was that one Sunday in October a newspaper ran a shocking story, alleging that David had kissed and flirted with Page 3 girl Emma Ryan and even suggested they get a hotel room before deciding he couldn't go through with it because of his love for Victoria. It was complete nonsense and the pair laughed it off publicly, although Victoria later wrote in her autobiography about the pain it had caused. It also provoked more claims from another woman that were to prove unfounded.

It was an uncomfortable time in what had been an extraordinary year. Ever since they first got together, people had been asking of the couple, were they really so genuinely in love? The answer is yes, but, in a rather ugly display of Schadenfreude, there was a certain degree of delight from some quarters that the perfect couple were not all they seemed. As a matter of fact they were, but it caused some unhappiness for Victoria at the time. Ultimately, however, it was to draw the two yet closer together.

As the tumultuous year drew to a close, David continued to play ever better as well as fitting in a short break with Victoria in Marbella, where he was seen publicly kissing Victoria's tummy. And the show ran on much as before. David continued to experiment with new looks – a beard made an appearance in November – and continued to sign lucrative sponsorship deals, the latest being with Pepsi. There was another brief moment when it looked as if David was allowing his temper to run riot again during a clash with Blackburn skipper Tim Sherwood, but David had finally learned his lesson and the fracas was a one-off.

And by the end of the year Beckham had finally regained his footballing crown – and was the better player for it. That which does not destroy us makes us stronger and David had been through a patch that would have brought down a lesser man. However, his innate maturity, so much in evidence when he was younger, combined with the strength of his relationship with Victoria, saved him from the abyss. David had emerged a stronger man.

'There is no way I could have survived the World Cup aftermath without Victoria,' he said. 'That's why I went straight to New York to be with her. She didn't say a word when I saw her, just gave me a big cuddle. She was about a month pregnant – no one knew except us – and was as pleased to see me as I was to see her. No way did I expect things to turn as nasty as they did but, once I was with her, I knew I'd get through it.'

Eventful as this year had been, the next was to be equally full of drama. David was to become a father and a husband, in that order, and celebrate a wedding that overshadowed even that of Prince Edward and Sophie Rhys-Jones. But it was not all to be plain sailing for, as David's fame and popularity was to soar ever higher, one man was increasingly dismayed by the turn of events. That man was Sir Alex Ferguson.

Chapter Seven

Super Becks

It was a typical Beckham start to the new year: David celebrated the arrival of 1999 by buying a new £150,000 silver Ferrari 550 Maranello. It was a beautiful car, fit for a famous footballer – although, as onlookers observed, it was a two-seater with nowhere to store the nappies. No matter, David had come through a very difficult year and clearly felt he deserved a little present to cheer himself up.

He was playing well, with no major upsets, but there did seem to be a slight change in his lifestyle. Beckham had always loved clothes and revelled in being a fashion icon but, now more than ever, he seemed to be entering into Victoria's world. The two were pictured for *Vogue*, lying entwined around each other and with Victoria's seven-month bump clearly visible. Victoria gave an interview to accompany the pictures, in which she said she would carry on working after the baby's birth in March. 'I'll just take the baby straight into the studio with me.' And what would she do at night? 'Straight in a cot, although I have heard there are some babies who never sleep … aren't there?' The couple were in for a rude awakening.

The interview gave a very revealing portrait of a very close couple, with Victoria expressing herself in her usual, inimitable way. Explaining that she nearly had his and hers loos put in the master bedroom she continued, 'I've weed in front of David right from the beginning, but then we've always been more like friends. Well, looks aren't going to last forever, are they?'

It got better. Reminded that the in your face TV pundit Jeremy Clarkson had said he'd like to get David alone in a padded cell after the World Cup fiasco, Victoria mused, 'A lot of people would have topped themselves over that.' She gave David a hug. 'But don't worry, I'll look after you. Just send him round here, *I'll* beat him up.'

She was clearly on superb form, describing the Alderley Edge apartment's decor as 'a cross between a poof's house and a whore house'. Life consisted of walking the dog and snuggling up on the sofa to watch *Friends* and the two even went to the local Tesco. 'It's fine. They're very posh round where we live,' said Posh. 'If anyone wants an autograph I say, "Not until we're finished," and then I get all the children to line up and tell them that if they don't say please they're not going to get one. David and I were talking about this the other day, weren't we? We want children who are very well behaved.' It was Victoria – and David – down to a T.

To mark Valentine's Day, David gave Victoria a picture of the couple embracing: Victoria was so thrilled that she promptly ordered another one for the nursery. David then went on record to address Glenn Hoddle's accusation, namely that he was not sufficiently focused on the game.

'Personally, I didn't agree with that comment about me not being focused,' he said. 'I've been brought up to believe that, whether you're playing on Hackney Marshes or in the World Cup, you give it everything you've got. My dad, my Sunday league managers – especially one called Stewart Underwood almost 20 years ago – and now Alex Ferguson have always stressed that to me. I don't start focusing when the whistle goes, I start on the Wednesday before Saturday's match or sooner.'

The wounds from that shattering time had clearly not entirely healed. 'It was frustrating not to play in the first two games when I was so keen to do my best for my country,' he went on. 'My feelings never seemed to matter. I want to stress that I'm always happy to respect a manager's wishes but I was very keyed up by the time I got to play and I think things might have turned out differently if I'd played in those two games.' It was the closest David had ever got to blaming Glenn Hoddle for the whole debacle.

David was also keen to clarify his attitude towards his own celebrity. 'I can see how the public or football fans might think I'm letting things slip or getting distracted by celebrity nonsense but what they don't understand is that I can't step out of the front door without getting photographed – and what happens in 10 seconds of my life can stay in the papers for a month,' he said. 'I'm not flash. I like nice things and a nice lifestyle – not because they portray an image to the outside world but because they make me happy. But nothing distracts me from my football.'

He talked avidly of his happiness with Victoria. 'I've got the girl of my dreams, the job I always wanted, a baby on the way and marriage round the corner,' he said. 'There are so many good things in my life that the black moments never last long. All the criticism can fly straight over my head if I've got her to come home to. I started thinking about proposing to her about a week after we met. She came on to me, actually, but I'd had a funny feeling about Victoria before I'd even met her. I saw her on the telly and thought that, if I could just meet her once, we'd be together forever.

'I'm totally ready for fatherhood. I'm so over the moon I'm lost for words. The happiest moment of my life was when she told me she was pregnant and, although it wasn't planned, there wasn't a split second of doubt in my mind. We both understand what it involves and we're both ready for the responsibility – but then we'd better be, it's due in three weeks. I know a lot of things have been said about us being too young and not married, and being bad role models for young people. But we love each other, we're best friends and we're ready to be parents. I think that's a good example to set.'

The subject of David's football career arose and it makes ironic reading now. 'I have no great desire to play abroad, but you can never say never,' he said. 'United might get sick of me and sell me abroad or to London, but I want to stay at United for the rest of my career and continue to repay the debt I owe to the boss, the club and the best fans in the world. After that, management holds no appeal for me. What I would really like to do is open a school of excellence for kids – boys *and* girls. It's not a normal ambition for a footballer but it's something I've always wanted to do. A lot of people helped me to get where I am and I want to put something tangible back into the game.'

Did Beckham really say 'girls'? 'It's something I feel strongly about,' said David, going into full new-man mode. 'I think it's important to remove the idea that football is an exclusively male domain. When I was at school, some of the girls were as good as the boys and getting them involved more might help to remove some of the macho nonsense that mars the game.'

Sir Alex's reaction to that is not on record – but it can certainly be imagined.

As David prepared for fatherhood, there was another ordeal to be faced – Diego Simeone, the player whose antics got David sent off in the World Cup. The two were to meet at Old Trafford when Simeone's team, Inter Milan, came to play at Old Trafford and it was a reunion that was expected to be tense. Simeone attempted to extend an olive branch before the match. 'I want to make it known that I respect David Beckham and all of his Manchester United teammates,' he said. 'I have a lot of admiration for him as a footballer. He is a fantastic player. One of United's greatest strengths is their crosses, and Beckham and Ryan Giggs can pose problems for any fullback. They test the best defences.

'It is not for David Beckham to feel guilty over his sending off at the World Cup and what happened after it. This is football – the same thing has happened to me. The referee believes you have done something wrong and you must go off. I know what has been said but these are the facts: Argentina won the match against England because we beat them in a penalty shootout. That is all, no other reason. Such a thing can not be the fault of one player. As far as I am concerned, our duel is history. That was the World Cup and this is the Champions League and Inter is all that matters to me now.'

David did not reply.

Simeone made matters still worse when he

confessed to overreacting during the match. 'Let's just say the referee fell into the trap,' he told an Italian newspaper. 'It was difficult for him because I went down well and, in moments like that, there's lots of tension. My falling transformed a yellow card into a red card. In reality, it wasn't a violent blow, it was just a little kick back with no force behind it.' These were words that were scarcely likely to endear him to United fans – let alone to David himself.

David got his revenge. United beat Inter Milan 2–0, with David setting up Dwight Yorke for the two goals. Alex Ferguson was delighted. 'Beckham is back to his best,' he said. 'They could not handle him or Dwight Yorke. I didn't say anything to David about Simeone before he went out. I didn't need to. I think he is an outstanding central midfield player. But he is also the best crosser of a ball in Europe. And, until I find someone who can cross a ball as well, he will stay out on the right.'

David, meanwhile, was gracious in his triumph. He and Simeone actually embraced and exchanged shirts before David went to acknowledge the rapture from the crowd.

One of the fans watching was Simply Red star Mick Hucknall, who was fulsome in his praise for David after the game. 'I only ever really deal with the media when I've got a new album,' he said. 'David is under much more pressure than I ever am, and I can only admire him for the way he deals with it. After the

Argentina game it could all have gone horribly wrong for him. Some of the chants, the things rival fans were saying to him were appalling. Even now some of them still boo him. But he has adopted the right attitude. He is set a great example by Alex, who handles everything so professionally.

'But he still deserves a great deal of credit for the way he has focused any anger and frustration on to football. Last night I was so impressed by the way he performed. Not only did he provide two brilliant crosses but he was also defending and tackling. He was all over the park. My respect for David went up tenfold for the commitment he showed and the gesture he made by swapping shirts with Simeone. It was brilliant and showed real maturity.'

It was a fitting end to the drama and, as if to acknowledge a new beginning, Victoria went into labour the very next day. She was taken to London's Portland Hospital where, on 4 March 1999, she gave birth to the couple's first child, a 7lb boy named Brooklyn Joseph Beckham. He was called Brooklyn because that's where Victoria was when she found she was pregnant, while Joseph is both David's middle name and the name of one of his grandfathers.

David was absolutely delighted. 'Victoria is very well,' he told assembled reporters outside the hospital. 'She is sitting up drinking champagne. I'm feeling very well, I'm over the moon – it is something I have always wanted to do. It's a new experience for me. It's the best thing that's ever happened to me. It's unbelievable – it's something that can't be beaten. The birth was natural and there were no complications, nothing at all. Victoria might be here for a couple more days.'

A succession of visitors included Emma Bunton and Victoria's parents and brother and sister, while Spice Girls fans kept vigil outside the hospital. It then emerged that, in fact, there had been a slight complication – Victoria was forced to have a Caesarean when doctors discovered that Brooklyn was in the wrong position. But it was a time of great rejoicing for David and the start of a period that was going to turn him into possibly the most famous father in Britain.

Victoria stayed in the hospital for five days, after which the new family made a getaway in true Hollywood style. A limousine with blacked-out windows pulled up at the Portland's goods entrance, Victoria and David clambered inside with Brooklyn and the car roared off with a police escort to Victoria's parents' home in Goff's Oak. Later, David emerged to make a statement: 'We just want to be on our own, just the three of us,' he said. 'The baby is lovely, sitting in his mum's arms. I am very pleased. Victoria's fine, naturally she's a bit tired, but she's sitting with him in her arms – it's great.'

Other family members also spoke of their happiness. Victoria's sister Louise said, 'He's fast asleep. It's lovely to have them home and Victoria's so pleased to be back with her family.'

Meanwhile, Jackie Adams, Victoria's mother, said, 'The baby is lovely. It's good to be a grandma.'

It is noteworthy, though, that David's parents weren't there. They had been present at the hospital when Victoria gave birth and had already seen their new grandson, but it was with her own parents that Victoria chose to spend the following weeks. From the very earliest days that David and Victoria were together, their life outside football tended to revolve around her parents rather than his. The Adams family spoke warmly about welcoming David into their midst, but in doing so it is possible that David's parents felt left out.

Logistically, it made sense for the couple to spend their time at Goff's Oak, for the simple reason that Victoria's parents were better off than David's and thus had a bigger house, but, even so, a picture was beginning to emerge. David was entering Victoria's world rather than vice versa and it was to lead to David's father Ted talking with some regret about growing apart from his famous son.

With his home life so secure, David was beginning to put the events of the past year into perspective. Glenn Hoddle had recently published an account of the World Cup, in which he revealed that he ignored David after the game, believing it would be best to leave him alone – a decision that David found deeply wounding. 'When

I was shown the red card, I was really gutted,' he said. 'More than anything I wanted to play the rest of the game. That was the only thing I was really thinking about – and the team winning, of course.

'I was sat outside the changing room afterwards when Tony Adams came over. He sat down with me and he was brilliant. I will remember that because that was what I needed at the time. The manager didn't actually speak to me after the game. Not at all. My family and friends were the only people who wanted to talk to me.'

But David conceded that he had learned a great deal from the whole experience. 'It made me grow up a lot,' he said. 'It has made me realise a few things, although I feel that with everything that happened after the World Cup I was treated unfairly. I think the majority [of fans] dislike me. I don't know whether it's jealousy or not, but I think there are more people who don't like me than like me. I'd like to be really popular, but I don't think that is going to happen now.' David was being overly modest. While there would always be fans who would heckle him – probably because they were jealous – the public as a whole was beginning to warm to him as never before.

And what could be better to celebrate Brooklyn's birth than winning a high-profile match? United beat Chelsea 2–0 a few days later, and while both goals were scored by Dwight Yorke, he paid tribute to David after the first one by making a baby-rocking sign with his arms. David was delighted – and later revealed that he'd been a little weary before the match, due to baby-watching duties. 'I was a little bit tired on the morning of the match because I was up all night with him,' he confessed. 'But I had a good sleep at the hotel in the afternoon and I enjoyed the game.'

Despite David's public comments about the hurt he'd felt at the hands of Glenn Hoddle, the England manager was also generous in his praise. 'He's got good support around him and it's not only good to see him playing excellently, but also that his family life's going well, too,' he said. 'If people leave him alone, I'm sure he's going to go from strength to strength.'

Brooklyn made his first public appearance, fittingly enough, on Mother's Day. Ten days after the birth, David, Victoria, Brooklyn and the entire Adams family, plus Louise's daughter Liberty, went out en masse to celebrate at the Down Hall Country House Hotel in Bishop's Stortford. Victoria was clearly regaining her figure – in fact, the world had seen the last of the more rounded Victoria of the Spice days as she was to go on to lose an enormous amount of weight - and was looking svelte. 'I'm really happy to be with my family and a great time was had by all,' she said as the group left the restaurant. Motherhood was clearly suiting her.

Ferguson, though, was leaving David in no doubt that he was expected to carry on as usual. Despite admitting to tiredness, he played in all five of United's matches in the two weeks after Brooklyn's birth and by the time the team played Everton in late July he was beginning to look exhausted. However, he pulled himself together in the second half, scoring a magnificent goal and leading his team on to a 3–1 victory. Even Sir Alex was impressed.

The couple were clearly weary, but they were determined to bring Brooklyn up without extra help. On top of that, David was new man incarnate. 'We had a child so we can raise him, not a nanny,' said Beckham. 'I love looking after Brooklyn. In fact, I've just changed a nappy. We both get up with him in the night and Victoria's really good with Brooklyn, very motherly. She never leaves his side and she feeds him and washes his clothes – that's the way she wants it.

'We're a family now and I'm the happiest I've been in a long time. Since we've had Brooklyn, I've grown up a lot and he's made me look at life from a new perspective. If something winds me up at work I come home and take a look at what we've made together. Things that were important before just don't seem as important now. I cried when he was born. I wanted to cut his umbilical cord, but the doctor did it so quickly I didn't get the chance. He's got Victoria's nose and colouring but he's starting to go blond like me. He's got my legs, my feet and my toes – exactly the same toes as me.'

And David went on to reveal that he frequently drove through the night after matches to get back to his wife-to-be and child, and sped back to them after a recent match. 'I was tired but I hate being away from them,' he said. 'I absolutely hate it. It was 3am when I got there but I was quite happy to sit up all night just watching Brooklyn breathe. He's beautiful – different every day. He eats unbelievably, so he's gaining weight all the time. And he has started smiling, too – especially when he's got wind!'

Brooklyn was already being introduced to his parents' lifestyle. He was taken to a shopping centre by Victoria about three weeks after he was born and was spotted at London's exclusive restaurant The Ivy, dining in the company of Sir Elton John, no less. There was some amusement over his parents' appearance, given that they were still coping without a nanny: both appeared to be sleepwalking.

But, be that as it may, both were also deliriously happy. 'We'd like a couple more,' said David. 'But I don't think I'd be able to fit any more names on my football boots. I usually have Beckham printed on the front of my boot, but now it's Brooklyn, with Beckham at the back. I think the sponsors Adidas are quite pleased.' He was quoted in an interview with *Time Out* magazine, the front cover of which caused quite a stir in itself. David was pictured on the cover wearing all white, with a rosary around his neck and his arms out in a supplicating pose. The cover was entitled, 'The Resurrection Of David Beckham'. The image would have been controversial at any time, but, given that it was in the run-up to Easter, Church leaders were not best pleased.

'I think everybody has to be careful playing with symbols that are important to other people,' said a spokesman for the United Reform Church. 'These things shouldn't be walked all over.'

Meanwhile, the Church of England's director of communications, Dr Bill Beaver, said it was 'unfortunate' that Beckham should allow himself to be pictured thus.

Meanwhile, David and Victoria were beginning to prepare for their summer wedding. After months of indecision, the two finally decided to marry in Ireland, at a spectacular venue called Luttrellstown Castle. The venue was just outside Dublin and the ceremony, which was to be covered by *OK! Magazine* in a £1-million deal, was to take place on 4 July, exactly four months after Brooklyn's birth.

Wedding invitations were sent out featuring a crest of arms, which the two had chosen for themselves – and which provoked some snorts of mirth from heraldry experts. Neither could have cared less. Victoria gave an interview to *OK!*, in which she talked about her happiness. 'All I was interested in was having a healthy baby,' she said. 'It's just amazing how much you can love another person.'

David, meanwhile, was still brooding on the pain of separation. 'It's really hard being away from the baby,' he said. 'I just want to spend every minute of the day with him. You want to be there, you want to see every little movement, every little thing that he does differently.'

As the wedding preparations continued, there was intense speculation as to whether Geri Halliwell would be invited. David and Victoria had seen her briefly when they all had dinner in the South of France, but relations between the remaining Spice Girls and the one who walked out had become increasingly strained. In the event, there was no invitation. 'I don't even want to comment on how I feel about it,' snapped Geri at a press conference.

Victoria, meanwhile, was claiming that hardly anyone would be invited. 'David and I haven't got that many friends. We could have our wedding in a postbox if we wanted to,' she joked to Zoe Ball on Radio 1.

There was also an enormous amount of curiosity about the wedding dress. Victoria stayed coy. 'I went with Mum [to try the dress on] and we were all girlie and it was great,' she said. 'It isn't a Versace dress, there's been a lot of rumours and it isn't.'

In the run-up to the big day, David and Victoria gave an interview to *OK! Magazine*, which took place in their Cheshire flat. The flat itself was pretty much what you would expect from a Spice Girl and a footballer. There was a huge portrait of the couple by Jurgen Teller hanging in their entrance hall, and high church candles on either side of the door. The rest of the flat was also littered with candles. The kitchen was home to a fake leopard-print scatter rug, radiators shaped like ladders and a huge Miele oven; the bathroom housed an enormous bath, double shower and matching his and hers Versace robes and towels; and in the sitting room there was a four-foot elephant, side tables and a collection of Buddhas and other statues. There were wooden floors throughout and white painted walls, covered with photographs of the couple.

The two were clearly blissfully happy and spoke openly about Brooklyn's birth and their life together. Talking about her dash to hospital, Victoria said, 'Basically, the baby's head was not in place and it would never have been, so I had a Caesarean, which was very last minute. You have a choice – you can go into labour, but if the head still doesn't engage, you end up having an emergency Caesarean, which can make the baby stressed.

'All I was interested in was having a healthy baby, and it's funny how suddenly your mind begins to work and all your priorities change. It was like when I was actually in the theatre, I said to David, "If they take the baby away, for whatever reason, just leave me here, half-dead or whatever, and just go with the baby – make sure you don't let him out of your sight." But all the doctors were absolutely fantastic, the hospital, the staff … Mr Gillard, who actually delivered Brooklyn, was amazing and you can't even see my scar!'

Was David there? 'I couldn't watch the actual operation,' he revealed, 'but Mr Gillard said, "The head's halfway out if you want to look now," and, just as I looked up, he was pulling Brooklyn's head out, he opened his eyes ... unbelievable! I just cried.' Did his father offer advice? 'He's not really like that, my dad,' David continued. 'All we talk about is football! No, a couple of nights before Brooklyn was born he did take me to one side and said, you know, when the baby's born, when you first set eyes on him, you'll understand how we feel about you. And my mum absolutely loves babies, so she just couldn't wait.'

David was also asked if his parents were advising him to slow down a bit. 'No!' he replied. 'My mum and dad know Brooklyn and Victoria are the most important things in my life – but they also know how dedicated I am to playing football and to Manchester United.' And, it was pointed out, David put a lot of work into his relationship, while working in a field not known for its sensitivity. 'There's other working environments where people have that reputation, too,' said David calmly. 'The fact is that this is the first time I've ever been in love. I think, once you meet that person you want to spend the rest of your life with, you know and, no matter what else is going on around you, you dedicate your life to that person. You'd never hurt or destroy that relationship.'

A couple of days later, Victoria celebrated her 25th birthday by taking Brooklyn to watch United playing Sheffield – only for David to be left on the bench. But Brooklyn had now seen his father's working environment – something that he was destined to do a great deal more. 'I really wanted Brooklyn to see his dad play but he seemed to enjoy the noise and the atmosphere afterwards,' he said. 'I'm sure that he'll be coming back for more now that he's got his first game out of the way.' He might also have enjoyed the sight of 'Happy Birthday Victoria' flashing across the scoreboard.

Nothing was too much for David to do to show his devotion to his newborn son. He had the name 'Brooklyn' tattooed along the lower half of his back, although it must be said that, should the couple turn out to have a large family, there probably won't be room for many more.

There was a brief health scare when Victoria discovered a lump in Brooklyn's stomach when she was changing him, but it turned out to be an umbilical hernia that had to be removed. 'It's a routine op and the doctors have said not to worry,' said a spokeswoman for Victoria. 'Any new parents are concerned if they have to take their baby to hospital. But David and Victoria have been assured that it's a common operation.'

Brooklyn safely returned to health and with David newly named by *France Football* magazine as the second-highest-paid footballer in the world after Ronaldo – Becks was now estimated to be earning £3 million a year – everything in the garden should have been rosy. But, as ever, there were rumblings of discontent in the background. For a start, rumours continued that Victoria was not happy living in the north and that she wanted David to move to another football team. Victoria denied it, but the couple still admitted that their Cheshire home was not permanent and that they were looking to buy a whole house in the south.

And, as ever, there was the constant worry about whether Sir Alex was still happy with his protégé. Brooklyn's birth had only intensified interest in the couple, on top of which David's publicity was now being looked after by Outside Organisation. These were the Spice Girls' agents and it was at Victoria's behest that David put his business with them. Sir Alex was saying nothing – for now.

As for David and Victoria, they didn't have time to worry, for they had something much more interesting on their agenda. They had a summer wedding to plan.

Chapter Eight

The Becks a Man Can Get

Preparations for the wedding were now in full swing. Luttrellstown Castle found itself at the centre of attention, to the extent that security guards were employed to prevent curious fans sneaking in to find out what was going on. The castle itself boasted 14 bedrooms, reception rooms including the Van Stry Room, named after the Dutch painter and adorned with his paintings, and a dining room called the Kentian room. It had a ceiling painted in 1753 by Jacob de Wit of The Triumph of Bacchus and Ceres.

David turned 24 in May and celebrated with a quiet party at the couple's Cheshire home. Shortly afterwards he assured fans for the umpteenth time that he had no plans to quit United. 'I never had any doubts about staying,' he said. 'I think, at the start of the season, a lot of people were wondering whether I would crack. Or whether I would go abroad. But all I wanted was to come back to United and to be playing again. That was important for me. The manager told me, "As long as you get back here and get playing for us again, then you will be fine." And I have been pleased by the way it's gone for me since then.

'At times it has been hard getting that reaction from the crowds, but the lads here have been brilliant for me. I couldn't have asked for more support. And I never had any doubts about staying. I knew I was going to get stick when I went to away grounds. I've had that every away game. But I'm playing for the biggest club in the world so I expect that. You learn as you go along and it makes you a much stronger person.' The wounds of the previous year, although healing, were still clearly not entirely cured.

Victoria, meanwhile, launched an appeal for the Meningitis Research Foundation in London. Having just had a health scare with Brooklyn, by now nine weeks old, she was increasingly aware of the fears faced by new parents, and admitted to being constantly worried about Brooklyn. 'Brooklyn is the most important thing in the world to us,' she said. 'The thought of anything happening to him is a complete nightmare. I wake up in the night in a panic. I don't know what I think might have happened to him, but I love him so much. Until you're a mother, you don't know how hard it all is.'

Brooklyn, she said had, recovered 'brilliantly' from his recent operation. 'He's fine,' she went on. 'He smiles a lot and is aware of everything around him. We're going to be like the Waltons and have a house full of children and dogs. I definitely want to have a lot more children now that I've had him. We take it in turns to do everything, he [David] bathes Brooklyn as much as I do.'

Finally, after months of speculation, Victoria's choice of wedding-dress designer was revealed: Vera Wang. The American-based designer was a surprise choice, but she certainly had form when it came to dressing celebrities, numbering Sharon Stone and Mariah Carey among her clients. 'I'd seen her work previously – other celebrities she'd dressed – and I'd always really respected her,' said Victoria.

'But I thought she was such a nice lady, open to ideas, which I think is important. There are certain little things I'd like to put on the dress and she's really open to that. I couldn't work with anyone who's got a big ego and won't listen to anyone else's opinion. It is an exciting time when you are planning a wedding and it is nice to have people who are excited about it as well.'

David was equally excited about the wedding and was also resigned to the fact that he was still hero or zero, depending on who you talked to. As United prepared for their FA Cup Final against Newcastle and the European Champions Cup Final against Bayern Munich, he revealed that he had only recently seen pictures of the effigy that had been hung outside the pub. 'I only saw a picture about four months ago,' he said. 'A grown man doing something like that is pathetic. I knew the United fans would be behind me and I think I'm playing more consistently for my club and my country.

'But you see the papers and what people are saying on the telly,' he continued, sounding slightly more aggrieved than usual. 'One minute they wanna hang you, the next you're gonna win the game against Luxembourg – my "comeback game". There's never been a point where I thought, 'Right, I've won them over', because I don't think I ever will. The papers are probably writing nicer things about me, but there's still time in my career for them to change their minds again!'

His personal feelings certainly didn't affect his football. United won the FA Cup final against Newcastle, with Ferguson singling out David for praise, after which they went on to trounce Bayern Munich. The club was now being spoken of as one of the greatest ever, with Beckham in particular increasingly being cited as a truly great footballer. Such was his prowess that the fans were even prepared to overlook his new-mannishness, his frequent declarations of love for Victoria and Brooklyn, his modelling sessions and his love of fashion.

Even more unusually for a footballer, David was also frequently cited as an icon by the gay community, something, he said, that flattered him – and there aren't many footballers who would be willing to say that. David, in fact, was becoming something extraordinary: not only a truly brilliant footballer, but a truly modern icon for our times. He wears make-up, he hardly even notices when people tease him about it, he cries unashamedly at events like his son's birth, he cooks, he treats Victoria superbly well and there aren't even any vices in the background like smoking and excessive drinking. If you were to make up all the ingredients for a role model for today, you would come up with David Beckham – and no one would believe that one man could be so perfect.

Also, he was a pretty good footballer. Cradling the Champions Cup after the Bayern Munich match, David yet again vowed his loyalty to the club, not least because he knew he was an increasingly attractive proposition to other European clubs. 'I always want to be a Manchester United player, of course I do,' he said exultantly. 'When you do things like winning the European Cup, why would you want anything else? Why go anywhere else? It couldn't possibly get better wherever I went.

'I'll play whatever position the manager wants me to. I have no problem with that – whether it's the centre or wide right. The enjoyable part of being a footballer is playing week in, week out, and that's all I can ask for. I have never wanted to be out of the side and I haven't felt in need of a rest. It's been a tough season of hard work, but when you end up with three trophies, as we have, you know all the hard work has been worth it. You can't better it, of course, but you can repeat it and this win gives us the incentive to go on and look to the future because we want to win all three again.'

It was practically a declaration of love to Manchester United. At that point, the great question was not whether Sir Alex would sell David, but whether Beckham would leave of his own accord. And David, a man of integrity, wanted to make it absolutely clear where his loyalties lay. The only problem – in Ferguson's eyes if in no one else's – was that he had another life, a very different life, in the south of England. And Sir Alex was beginning to think that perhaps the two would not mix.

But others were not so concerned. Kevin Keegan had briefly taken over as England coach from Glenn Hoddle after Hoddle sparked a row when airing his views on reincarnation, and Keegan was impressed. 'We've got a lot of captains in the side,' he said, 'and David has shown true leadership qualities recently. We all saw them against Bayern Munich.' It was a hint of more glories to come.

David was also beginning to realise that, against his own expectations, he was winning the public round. Girls fancied him, men admired him and children wanted to be him. It was quite a change from the previous year and David was loving every minute of it. 'I love having little kids look up to me and young players looking up to me and respecting me,' he crowed. 'That's something I always did as a youngster when I looked up to great players like Bryan Robson and Bobby Charlton. That's exactly how I want to be looked at. I don't want to be looked at with people saying horrible things about me off the pitch, either.'

David was also very sensible about his relationship with the media. The world of celebrity is filled with people who would sell their own grandmother to get their picture in the paper and then complain about the intrusion of privacy, but David was not one of them. He was straightforward and open about it and he didn't complain. Quite the opposite. 'At the moment, everything is perfect,' he said. 'That's a nice feeling to have. We've won the treble, I'm in the England squad, playing regularly – and, of course, my private life is perfect, too, with my new little boy.

'I think you do grow up when you have kids. People said that to me, but I've just started to realise it now. It's the best feeling in the world. I think if you go through an experience like I did after last summer you can either crack up or you can come out and make people eat their words. I feel that's what I have done. There were a lot of things said that I didn't care about, but it was worse for my mum and dad than it was for me. I don't get any privacy, only in my own home when the curtains are closed. Apart from that, that's it. There are so many people trying to get into my life and have a piece of me but I've come to learn to accept that. It's gone on for the whole year since the summer. But I've got on with it and grown up and I'm enjoying things.'

The euphoria couldn't last and there was, indeed, a blip: England drew 0–0 against Sweden, putting hopes of qualifying for the Euro 2000 finals on a knife edge. It didn't help that David pulled a hamstring and was thus unable to play in the next match. But everything else was going so well in his life that it hardly seemed to matter. The wedding was now less than a month away and David and Victoria were spotted carrying on business as usual: they were pictured going shopping in London's Knightsbridge – with David flashing the cash quite as much as his bride-to-be.

Beckham's parents were understandably delighted with all the praise and good fortune being heaped on their talented boy. Ted was asked if he'd felt let down by David's actions in the previous year's World Cup. 'No, not at all – it's only a game of football, after all – but I know that David felt he'd let his teammates down,' he said. 'After the game, we went up to him and cuddled him. I think he was upset for the older players, because he knew they wouldn't get another chance to play in the World Cup. Everybody was upset with David, but to slaughter a player like the press did is beyond me. More could have been done to protect him.'

Sandra went on to talk about what David was like as a little boy. 'He was a bit of an artist,' she said, 'always drawing cartoon characters. I've kept all his old sketchbooks. And he was very tidy and would make his own bed every day. Even now he can't stand mess. He was never naughty – except for the time he got his ear pierced when he was 14. He'd asked me if he could do it and I'd said no, because it could be dangerous if he'd got his earring caught on something when he was playing football. But he did it anyway. He came in the front door and ran straight upstairs, so I knew something was wrong. I let him keep the earring in, but he soon decided he didn't like it any more and stopped wearing it.' It was a telling comment – the only time David had been naughty in childhood was over a fashion statement.

Ted went on to recall the time when David first became interested in football. 'I've always been a big football fan and a Manchester United supporter,' he said. 'As a young man I played football for Leyton Orient and Walthamstow. I used to run a Sunday league side and David used to come with me from the age of four or five. When the game was over, he and I would practise on the pitch together, kicking and shooting till half-past ten or eleven o'clock at night. I knew he was good. He had things I'd never seen in a little kid before – he had crossing ability and control. He never said he wanted to be anything else other than a footballer, and he always said that one day he was going to play for Manchester United.'

David was clearly destined to be a footballer right from the outset. Sandra went on to reveal more about David's abilities when he was little more than a toddler. 'We used to take lots of cine-films when David was little and in every one he's got a ball,' she said. 'We've got a film of him at 18 months, wearing a little Manchester United strip. We've kept all his United kits since then. From the age of seven, he used to play in the park across the road, where I knew he'd be safe. I had a friend who worked in the hut there, and I used to ring and tell her he was on his way so she could keep an eye on him.'

It also went without saying that David's other great interest as a child had been fashion. 'He always dressed very well,' said Ted. 'Whenever he asked for clothes for his birthday, it had to be a designer name. He was always good-looking and always quite popular with girls. He never went through an ugly-duckling stage, although I remember him being quite self-conscious when he lost his teeth.'

'As a child, David was quite short for his age,' added Sandra. 'When he went to Manchester United at the age of 16, he was smaller than me. I'm five foot four.' 'He shot up the following year,' said Ted. 'They must've put him in a growbag! I remember going to see him in Manchester and talking to Nobby Stiles. He used to say to me, "Don't worry, Mr Beckham, he'll be six foot one day." And he was right!'

Perhaps unsurprisingly, David was not an academic little boy. 'He didn't do much reading,' Sandra admitted, 'but he'd read former Man United captain Bryan Robson's autobiography, in which Bryan said he drank a raw egg mixture to help him build his strength. So he did that for a while.'

Did David's parents worry about the amount of publicity the two were attracting? 'Yes, for their sake,' said Sandra. 'I think it is really sad that they cannot just go for a walk with the baby, like we used to do with David and the others when they were young. David and Victoria both came along to Ted's 50th birthday party last year. We told all the guests not to ask them for photographs or autographs and nobody bothered them at all. They were able to dance and enjoy themselves, just do those little things which ordinary couples are able to do, but which they can't.'

That was, of course, the downside of their fame. But there was an upside, too, and a big one at that. While accepting that there was much they couldn't do that normal couples wouldn't even think about, the fact is that the pair of them love being famous – hence the tour of the United States in the summer of 2003, an attempt to crack the last country in which they were not instantly recognisable. And the two of them adore what their fame brings: beautiful clothes, fabulous houses and a jewellery collection that by this time must match that of the Queen, to name but a few of fame's advantages. David and Victoria are highly media savvy and fully aware that the day the cameras, the press et al lose interest is the day that they turn back into ordinary human beings. And they don't want that – and are honest enough to admit it.

Very unusually for such a famous couple, David and Victoria had an extremely strong support system: each other. Quite apart from the desire to remain famous, the two have an enormous amount in common and a bond that has simply grown and deepened as the years go by. The cynics who dismiss their relationship as a carefully cultivated media image could not be more wrong: it is utterly genuine. The two have found in each other that for which we all hanker: their other half. In this world of celebrity break-up and divorce – to say nothing of marital breakdown for the rest of us – it is sometimes easy to forget that there are genuinely devoted couples, and David and Victoria are just that.

Writer Rebecca Cripps, who has spent time with the couple, bears that out. 'David and Victoria's secret is that they never take each other for granted and are tuned into each other's emotional needs,' she said. 'They spend so long apart that they really cherish the time they have together. David writes her adorable little notes saying, "I love you", which he hides under her pillow, slips into her dressing-gown pocket or tucks in drawers where she will find them. And she has driven hundreds of miles just to spend 30 minutes with him.'

The wedding was drawing near. More details began to leak out: there were to be 340 guests, all of whom had been asked to wear black so that the bride and groom could stand out in white. Geri had found that she had other arrangements: she would be playing at the annual fundraising concert Party In The Park that Sunday. Victoria would be leaving the word 'obey' out of the service. David had installed a new £15,000 shower in the couple's Cheshire home. All right, that wasn't strictly wedding-related but the public hunger for snippets about the glamorous couple was now so strong that even the most trivial of details were lapped up. There was also intense speculation as to where they would be spending the honeymoon, with hotels all over the country claiming the bride and groom would be sleeping there.

And, in true new-man style, David cancelled his stag night in order to spend a quiet evening in with Victoria. He had been due to hit the town with Gary and Phil Neville, Nicky Butt and Paul Scholes, but at the last minute decided to stay in with Victoria instead. 'He told them he wanted to spend as much time with Posh and Brooklyn before the wedding as possible,' said a friend. 'He feels it is his duty to be as supportive as possible at the moment. Posh is excited but also very nervous. And she needs as much reassurance from David as brides-to-be usually need from their fiancés. It's not that she can't be without him for the night – it's more that he didn't want to be without her.

'He is very aware of his responsibility towards her and Brooklyn. And, to be honest, he prefers to spend time with them more than anyone else. Brooklyn had

143

that hernia operation a few weeks ago and he's teething now. So David felt he should put his role as a father first. Gary Neville is going to be his best man at the wedding anyway and Phil, Nicky and Paul will be there too. It's not like they minded. They are all great mates and understood entirely.'

In fact, the two could hardly bear to be away from each other at all. Victoria also had no plans for a hen night as she would rather have spent the time with David. 'She prefers to have a few close friends round to her home, cook a meal and have a laugh,' said the friend. 'That's what she will do instead of hitting the town. She and David are happiest when they are alone together. Even the idea of spending the night before the wedding apart isn't one they like. They'll both spend it with their parents, going through the final details. But no doubt they will get on the phone to each other.'

And, just temporarily at least, they enlisted the services of a nanny. They had hired Bentley's Entertainments to look after the wedding and the company was run by Peregrine Armstrong-Jones, half-brother of Lord Snowdon and his wife Caroline. 'I'm Posh Spice but you really are posh,' said Victoria brightly when they were introduced. They all got on so well together that the Armstrong-Joneses lent them their nanny to look after Brooklyn while preparations were ongoing.

The day before the wedding, the couple posed outside

Victoria's parents' front door in Goff's Oak. David, dressed in black jeans and a white vest, said that he was calm and relaxed, adding, 'I'm not at all nervous.'

'I am a bit shaky but OK,' said Victoria who was wearing a leather miniskirt slit to the thigh, before bursting into a fit of giggles.

Photographer Humphrey Nemar was present. 'I have been taking snaps of Posh for years but I've never seen her look so happy and beautiful,' he said. 'She genuinely looked radiant. David looked over the moon. But then he should – he's about to get hitched to one of the world's most beautiful women who's also worth a few quid.'

Later that day the couple and their families flew to Dublin on a private jet as their guests also began to assemble in Ireland. En route to the airport they also got a surprise: Victoria's father Tony had phoned Radio 2 to request a special song for his daughter. He told DJ Ed Stewart that the pair of them would be tuning in to the show and asked him to play the Stevie Wonder song 'Sir Duke'.

A ring of steel had been set up outside the castle, which only intensified speculation as to what was going on inside. The reception, it was said, was going to be costing at least £500,000, although no one yet knew what it was really going to be like.

At last, the big day loomed. The guests, including Sir Bobby Charlton and David Seaman, began arriving at Dublin airport, from where they were taken to the castle itself. Assorted footballers and Spice Girls mingled with personal friends of the couple, with everyone in excellent spirits. It was noted that, of all the footballers present, many were carrying golf bags, while their wives and girlfriends attempted to outdo one another on the glamour front. The local villagers around the castle pretended they weren't unduly bothered by the assembly of stars gathered in their midst but were clearly as excited as everyone else by this marriage of the worlds of football and showbusiness. And, at long last, it was time for the wedding of the year: that of David Beckham to Victoria Adams.

Chapter Nine

I Take Thee...

The sun dawned bright on 4 July 1999. Luttrellstown Castle had never looked more beautiful: it was a fairytale setting for what had been a fairytale romance. And now, finally, two years after they met, David Beckham and Victoria Adams were going to tie the knot.

Months of preparation had led up to the big day. Bentley Entertainments had been in charge of the planning, but the couple, especially Victoria, had also had a good deal of say. 'David and Victoria had a huge input right from the start,' said Peregrine Armstrong-Jones. 'The wedding has been 14? months in the planning, during which time the couple have been all over the world. Wherever they were, I would get samples, fabrics and plans to them and Victoria would often ring me fives times a day with ideas and questions.'

First, of course, they had had to find the right location. 'Victoria wanted somewhere really private and unique, somewhere green and leafy, deep in the countryside,' said Peregrine. 'Architecturally speaking, she didn't want anywhere too stuffy and she felt the castle had clean lines and grand proportions without being too imposing.' Once the locations had been chosen, David and Victoria then decided on a Robin Hood theme for the wedding, with lots of greenery, twigs, apples and fabric coloured burgundy, dark green and purple. They also had not one but two florists on hand: Simon Lycett, who did the flowers for *Four Weddings and a Funeral*, and John Plested, whose clients included the Queen.

The proceedings began at about three o'clock in the afternoon, as family members began to gather in the entrance hall of the castle. Fresh apples had been sewn into an ivy arrangement along the banisters, and the apples pierced to emit a sweet smell into the air. A leafy walkway led across the lawns to a huge marquee. 'I still can't believe it,' said Sandra Beckham, who was wearing a white Frank Usher suit. 'All the things we've talked about for months are actually here.'

Ted was equally bowled over. 'It's just something special – a fairytale,' he said. 'Victoria's an absolutely lovely girl and I feel very, very proud of the pair of them.' He was also enthusing about meeting Sir Bobby

Charlton. 'He was my absolute hero when I was a youngster and my favourite moment was when I got to meet him alongside David. He was everything I'd imagined he would be – and a bit more.'

In fact, just about everyone was overwhelmed. 'When I went into the marquee with Victoria earlier, the orchestra was rehearsing "Goodbye", a special version of the Spice Girls' Christmas hit and I got so emotional we had to have a bit of a cuddle,' said Victoria's father Tony. 'In fact, I got so emotional I had to take a bike out and cycle round the golf course to get over it! I didn't think I'd ever be emotional. I can be as hard as nails at times, but today – I mean this whole thing has been on the drawing board for so long and to see it coming together is very, very moving.'

By half-past three the bridesmaids – Victoria's sister Louise, her daughter Liberty and David's niece Georgina – appeared. The two little girls were dressed as woodland flower fairies, complete with wings and coronets, while Louise wore a dress by Chloé. It was a fitted cream corset decorated with copper and gold flowers and diamonds and a long cream skirt. All three bridesmaids had been given Tiffany diamond necklaces by the bride and groom. David's best man Gary Neville was given a Cartier watch while the usher, Victoria's brother Christian, received a Rolex. Finally, the rest of the Spice Girls arrived, plus Jimmy Gulzar and Phoenix Chi his daughter with Mel, and a fleet of Mercedes drew up in front of the castle to take the guests to the folly, where the marriage would actually take place. All the rest of the guests were only going to the reception.

The folly was a tiny chapel hanging above a stream, about 500 metres from the castle. 'The folly was a ruin and very cave-like when we found it, but Victoria loved the look of it,' said Peregrine. 'We had to do a lot of work to get it ready for the day – we had to bring builders in, put up scaffolding, lay a new floor and install power.'

The Bishop of Cork, the Right Reverend Paul Colton, was officiating at the ceremony. 'I don't see the ceremony as a marriage between two celebrities, but of a couple who are very much in love,' he said. 'They have had the same preparation and consultations as any other couple I have ever married.'

Victoria's dress, which she described as 'very Scarlett O'Hara', was in champagne-coloured satin, with a tight bodice and full skirt. Underneath it she wore a corset by Mr Pearl. Her shoes were also Vera Wang and on her head she wore a diamond and gold coronet by Slim Barrett. She was also wearing a beautiful diamond crucifix, which David had bought her for Christmas and which she had never worn before. David, meanwhile, was wearing a cream suit by Timothy Everett.

The couple had had rings designed by Asprey and Garrard. Victoria's was a marquise-set diamond supported on either side by three grain-set baguette diamonds and set in 18-carat yellow gold. David's was a full eternity ring, with 24 baguette diamonds and 24 smaller diamonds set in yellow gold. As a wedding present, David had given Victoria a pair of Asprey and Garrard emerald-cut diamond earrings set in 18-carat gold to match her ring, as well as a gold waist chain. Victoria gave him a Breguet watch.

Inside the folly itself, a string quartet had been entertaining the guests. But at 4.32 p.m., fashionably late, Victoria arrived on the arm of her father and waiting for her at the altar, with a sleeping Brooklyn in his arms, was David. Victoria walked up the aisle to the tune of Wagner's 'Bridal Chorus' from *Lohengrin* and the service began. 'They have chosen to be married according to the rites of the Church of Ireland and we are their supporters,' said the Bishop of Cork. David and Victoria smiled.

The reading, delivered by Reverend Lynda Peilow, was from John 15, 9–12: 'As the father has loved me, so I have loved you; abide in my love.' At this, David placed a kiss on Victoria's shoulder. After a short musical interlude, the Right Reverend Colton began his address. 'David and Victoria, Victoria and David, the marriage service doesn't give us a way of putting these names in order but, through your whole married life, you put each other first.' Everything about the service, every sight and sound was beautiful, he went on – 'except that', and gestured at a helicopter flying overhead.

But why do we do this, he asked. 'Why do we make everything so beautiful? It's simply because words fail us at a time like this. So we do all these beautiful things because they say better than words can: "Thank you" and "I love you". There is a lot of interest in this marriage and we are all excited to be here. But what matters is what is in David's heart and what is in Victoria's.'

The bishop warned against empty infatuation: 'The eyes that over cocktails seem so very sweet may not seem so amorous over Shredded Wheat,' which got a smile from Victoria. He then said that the key to a happy marriage was good communication, caring for people and 'finding a place for God and for spirituality in your lives'.

The couple were then called upon to face the congregation, where the banns were called. Since no one had any just cause or impediment to stop the wedding, he then put the couple's hands together before starting the marriage vows. At 4.49 p.m., the couple were pronounced man and wife. There was a whoop from the audience, cheers and clapping and a radiant David and Victoria kissed each other.

The newly married couple then knelt down at the altar and prayers were said: 'Almighty God, giver of life and love, bless Victoria and David, whom you have now joined in marriage. Grant them wisdom and devotion in their life together, that each may be to the other a strength in need, a comfort in sorrow and a companion in joy.' And then, just before 5 p.m., the couple walked up the aisle together to the tune of Mendelssohn's 'Wedding March'. Possibly the most famous couple in the world had been united in matrimony. 'It was very lovely,' said Victoria's sister Louise. 'I think everybody there was in tears.'

Back at the castle, the reception was getting under way. Guests were greeted by pageanters in Irish costume, while David and Victoria's crest flew on a flag above the castle. Inside was a 15-feet-tall floral arrangement, while guests were offered Laurent Perrier pink champagne, elderflower cordial with raspberries or Sicilian red orange juice. Canapés were also served before everyone made their way to the marquee. It had also been decorated in Robin Hood style: it was carpeted in deep red, while ivory taffeta adorned the sides. There were spectacular flower arrangements in burgundy, green and purple, and the tables were covered in dark green overlaid with cream linen calico and table decorations consisting of apples, candles and greenery. Moss-coloured candles were everywhere, and there were two huge chandeliers, also dressed in apples and greenery. 'It was a Robin Hood look meets Conran forest,' said Simon Lycett. David and Victoria themselves sat apart in their own private alcove, with Brooklyn in his favourite swinging chair at their side.

Dinner was a simple affair, as Victoria had already said she didn't want 'fiddled with' food. It consisted of tomato and red pepper soup, served in hollowed out pumpkins rather than bowls; chicken, asparagus, roast potatoes, French bean and sugar snap pea and herb jus; and then a choice of sticky toffee pudding with butterscotch (David's favourite) or summer berry terrine. In the background the 18-piece orchestra played a repertoire including the Spice Girls' hit 'Say You'll Be There' – the accompanying video to which afforded David his first sight of Victoria.

At 10.30 p.m. the couple cut the cake and speeches began. 'Ladies and gentlemen, many people would like to be here today but it is you that David and Victoria have chosen,' Tony Adams began. 'It is with great pride that I speak to you for a few moments about our bride and groom. Obviously, it is very difficult for me to find anything that hasn't already been written by the *News Of The World*, the *Sun*, the *Daily Mirror* – need I go on?'

Victoria, he continued, had never been any trouble. 'She started dance classes at the age of three and was soon rushing home from school to change from her uniform into a leotard to kick her legs about – little did she know that, only a few miles away, there was a little boy changing from his uniform into shorts to kick a ball around. They continued with enthusiasm and at 16 both left home to continue their training. Victoria went to dance college in Epsom and we all know where David went. As it happened, they both did quite well.'

Tony went on to describe how David saw Victoria on

video and how the two finally met, before ending, 'This afternoon I have given David someone who is very precious to me, but I know he will look after her, as he always does, with the utmost love and affection. We know we couldn't wish for a better son-in-law.' He asked guests to stand and wish 'our bride and groom a life of love and happiness – to the rest of the world they are Posh and Becks, but to us they are David and Victoria'.

Now it was David's turn. 'Thank you, Tony, for that speech – that meant more to us than you'll ever know,' he began. 'My wife and I' – that brought the ceiling down – 'would like to thank you for coming. I'm sure you'll agree that all the bridesmaids looked absolutely beautiful and stunning and I'd like to say that our mums have scrubbed up very well today, too! No, seriously, they look stunning.

'What can I say? My mother- and father-in-law have loved and supported me and been there for me and obviously that means the world to me. Jackie and Tony have given me something very precious to them. I will love and look after Victoria and treat her like a princess – which she always wants to be treated like.'

Turning to Victoria's brother, he continued, 'Christian, I've always wanted a brother and that's how I feel about you. And I feel just as close to Louise. I'd also like to thank my mum and dad who have brought me up from a young age – obviously! – and my sisters, who have been there from day one – obviously! Also, my nan and granddad who, in a few weeks, will be celebrating their 50th anniversary – I love you!'

And then it was a tribute to the best man. 'If Gary Neville's performances have been a bit shaky in the last few months, now you know why,' said David. 'He's been disappearing off to the toilet, wiping his brow and looking very worried. But Gary has always been there for me when I've needed him – especially when Victoria was away and I needed someone to talk to. I'd like to say that I really love you, Gary, and you'll notice we kiss a lot on the pitch!'

Finally, David turned to the most important people of all. 'This has been a massive year for us but she couldn't have given me a better present than the one she presented me with four months ago,' he said. 'I think "love" is a very strong word and all my love goes to Victoria and Brooklyn. Victoria wakes up every day and she seems to get more beautiful every time I see her. I know a lot of people say we've done it the wrong way around – had Brooklyn and then got married – but if you've got love, nothing else matters.'

And so, finally, to Gary Neville. 'He speaks well, that Julian Clary, doesn't he?' he began. Gary first thanked the bishop and everyone at the castle, then gave his apologies to the Spice Girls for the fact that Bayern Munich were not in attendance before saying he had a telegram from Diego Simeone – at which he held up a red card. Then there was a real telegram from Sir Alex Ferguson, who was attending another wedding elsewhere, various other messages of goodwill and finally something, 'from Prada, Gucci, Tiffany, British Telecom and Ferrari – best wishes and thanks for your support'.

Gary then talked about his friendship with David. 'David's outgoing and bubbly – I'm a bit of a moaning, miserable git,' he said. 'People are always asking me why I always kiss David Beckham. My answer is that I'd usually do much more than that to a six-foot blond in shorts with legs up to the armpits!' As for David's feelings about Victoria – 'He would come into training every day like a little schoolboy – you'd go a long way to find two people more madly in love.'

Finally, he turned to Victoria and told her she looked beautiful, before finishing, 'Brooklyn and Victoria have made David the happiest person in the world and that, in turn, has made me happy and everyone else in the room. Ladies and gentlemen – enjoy the evening and drink away!'

Everyone took him at his word. After dinner, the guests were led into a second marquee, which was decorated in Moroccan style, with luxurious gold and purple drapes and huge gold statues bearing flowers. The dance floor was painted in a black-and-white chequerboard design and surrounded by chaises longues and huge velvet and leopard-skin cushions with low-level tables.

David and Victoria slipped away and changed into their second outfits of the evening in matching purple designed by Antonio Berardi. Victoria's dress was what she termed a 'Jessica Rabbit' dress – a clinging, strapless gown of purple stretch satin, split to the thigh with a bright red lining. David was wearing a matching purple suit and had his hair up in a quiff – and even Brooklyn wore purple. The evening ended in riotous fun as the assembled footballers, Spice Girls and friends partied with a vengeance. The night was a triumph.

The whole affair was covered by *OK! Magazine* for £1 million and the two gave a lengthy interview afterwards. They first talked about choosing the venue. 'We spent a lot of time in Ireland when Victoria started her tour in Dublin and we felt at home here,' said David. 'The people are lovely – the photographers even asked our permission before they took a picture and, if we said. "No", they walked away.'

They were asked why they chose to marry in the folly. 'There isn't a church on the estate, so we had to find a location on the premises we could get licensed for a wedding ceremony,' said Victoria. 'We were just driving and we found the folly, which was in a complete state – a hermit had been living there. It was overgrown, half the floor was missing and there were big holes in the walls – it was like walking into a garden shed. But we just looked at each other and said, "This is the place." It was just big enough for our closest family and friends. I wanted the ceremony to be as private as possible.'

They were then asked if the celebrations were over the top. 'Whatever we do, we know we're going to get criticised,' said Victoria. 'Some people will say it's over the top. But then, if we'd had a small wedding, they would have said, "Couldn't they have done something bigger?" A lot of stuff is tongue-in-cheek. For example, we've got a flag on top of the castle with our initials, VDB, on it. We don't care what people say – as long as we're happy and our families are happy, that's all that matters.'

And why did David pick Gary Neville as his best man? 'Gary's been my closest friend since I moved to Manchester,' he said. 'I'm close to the whole team, but Gary's always been there when I've needed to talk to someone. We're the best of friends – I'm always round at his house. He was really pleased when I asked him to be best man. I know he's been very nervous about making his speech but he's a very good speaker at functions and I knew he'd be wicked.'

For a couple who were so often accused of flashiness, David and Victoria made an inspired choice when it came to wedding presents: they asked guests for vouchers for Marks & Spencer or Selfridges or suggested they made a donation to the Meningitis Trust. And would their relationship change once they were married? 'No, not at all,' said David. 'We've been a really close couple since day one. Obviously, Brooklyn's arrival has brought us closer together, definitely. There's three of us now and there's a lovely family atmosphere at home. Nothing could make us any closer than we already are.'

And so the wedding of the year, if not the decade, ground to a close. David was clearly blissfully happy: as a mature individual, being a family man clearly suited him. And he had married very well. Whatever the reservations of Sir Alex Ferguson and assorted others, Victoria was absolutely the right woman for him. Apart from the fact that they were and are absolutely besotted with one another, their union was to make the two of them one of the most famous couples on the planet. As individuals they had already made their mark but together they really were greater than the sum of their two parts. Victoria was already becoming more famous for her relationship with David than as a Spice Girl and as for David – his profile was to become so great that it actually overshadowed one of the most famous football clubs in the world.

But that was still to come. In the heady days after the marriage, the couple flew off to the South of France for a brief honeymoon to revel in being married and to calm down after all the excitement.

Back in Britain, however, there were rumblings of discontent from David's side of the family. Right from the start, the Beckhams had seen David becoming close to Victoria's family – indeed, he mentioned them before his parents in his bridegroom's speech – and now his great-uncle Peter, the brother of his grandfather, had his say. 'We hardly ever see David these days,' he said. 'It's such a shame. We used to be really close, but we have just drifted apart. He has changed since he met Victoria. That is what women do to men, isn't it?'

David and Victoria were learning the hard way that weddings could be as divisive among families as open warfare.

Warming to his theme, Peter, an electrician, continued, 'Don't get me wrong – Victoria is a lovely girl, generous almost to a fault and very shy, like David. But she's not necessarily the girl I'd have picked for my son. I'm not sure why things turned out the way they did. I think it's because the families are worlds apart. I've met Victoria's family. They think the world of David but we don't get on as well.'

The problem, it seemed, boiled down to class. Although Posh wasn't quite as posh as everyone initially thought, it was true that the Adams family had money and the Beckhams didn't. That was the root of the problem. 'Yet the Adams family are no different from anybody else except they've got a few bob extra,' said Peter. 'At the end of the day, they are just ordinary people with a famous daughter, like the Beckhams are ordinary people with a famous son.'

Peter had not been invited to the wedding. 'I was so disappointed – I've always understood weddings are for families,' he said. 'But the only people invited were David's parents, his sister, her fiancé and one uncle. Don't ask me why. Yet there were celebrities there with girlfriends they had only just met. I think it's wrong. Mind you, when I read about it, I wasn't quite as disappointed. That lavish display didn't fit in with what I know of David. It was rather extravagant and over the top – the word "tacky" springs to mind. But I think that's probably Victoria's influence, not David's.

'We've only seen his son Brooklyn once and that was accidental – we bumped into them in Marks and Spencers. We are disappointed we haven't seen more of him. I don't know why we haven't, although work obviously comes into it. Also, David's got a new life now. He's still extremely close to his parents, though.'

It was a harsh statement coming from a member of the family – and one who clearly felt left out. But what Peter failed to understand was that, in many ways, David and Victoria now needed only one another. Although they were close to their parents, their world was complete, especially now they had a child to bind them together. Friends of the couple speak of the fact that, when they're together, they are so absorbed in one another that they almost seem cut off from the world outside.

But the world outside continued to exist and it wasn't only David's family who had something to say about the wedding. The couple had hoped to honeymoon on an island in the Indian Ocean but had to opt for France instead when Sir Alex Ferguson refused to allow David to take off three days extra. The message was clear: it's fine to get married, but never forget that football comes first.

As autumn rolled on, the couple's profile continued to soar. They were interviewed for the September edition of *Vanity Fair* and appeared on the cover; the interview was notable not only for the sensuous pictures of the two of them rolling all over one another, but also for Victoria's defence of her husband's intellect. 'He's actually a really intelligent person,' she said. 'He's really deep, which I like. He's really frustrated because people think that, because he doesn't say a lot, he doesn't have a brain.' She went on to joke, 'We played Trivial Pursuit the other day and I was devastated – I got beaten by David Beckham!'

Victoria is spot-on about her husband's intelligence. Because David has, to put it bluntly, a silly voice, it's easy to credit him with less nous than he has. But, if you look at the evidence, you see a hugely rich man with a happy marriage, international profile and the maturity to cope with pressures that have all but destroyed the likes of Paul Gascoigne and George Best. David may not be a great intellectual but he possesses a wisdom denied not only to fellow footballers but most of the rest of us.

It is this wisdom that makes him such a likeable fellow and it also means he is totally unconcerned about matters that make other football stars go hot under the collar. That same autumn he was picked as part of an ideal gay team by the magazine *Attitude* for having 'the face of an angel and the bum of a Greek god'. David laughed it off. Even he, however, had his sang-froid tested in a match against Leeds at Old Trafford, making a V sign at the rival fans. For once, public opinion was completely behind him and he was not penalised: the fans had been jeering and making truly disgusting comments about Victoria and Brooklyn. A man's patience could only be tested so far.

And finally, after months of speculation, the couple bought what was to be their main home. Set in 24 acres of grounds, with an indoor swimming pool, the £2.5-million house was immediately and inevitably dubbed Beckingham Palace. The grounds contained ponds and an ornamental fountain; inside, the entrance hall contained an oak staircase and a magnificent chandelier. There was a huge dining room leading to the pool, an immaculate kitchen, breakfast room and study, along with seven bedrooms and an attached two-bedroom cottage. It was perfect and, even better, it was in Sawbridgeworth on the Hertfordshire – Essex border – close to both Victoria's parents and Stansted airport.

To celebrate, David bought a new car to add to his collection – a £92,000 Aston Martin DB7 to go with his Ferrari and Range Rover. He and Victoria also hit the town, prompting the usual concerns that his showbiz lifestyle would affect his football, not least when he appeared at a London party to launch Jade Jagger's jewellery collection less than 12 hours before he was due to fly out of Manchester with United to Austria.

Sir Alex was asked for his opinion and contented himself with a 'No comment'. However, his autobiography, *Managing My Life*, had recently been published, and in that he was more open about his feelings about Beckham. 'There was a period when I was troubled by the amount of travelling he was doing in his private life and about whether he was getting enough rest,' he wrote. 'Two or three trips a week to Ireland to be with Victoria was not an ideal preparation for what was being asked of him on the park and I had to stress that he had obligations to his own talent and his teammates. Fortunately, that is no longer a concern. Now Victoria and David have settled in Cheshire with their baby son Brooklyn, normal habits have been resumed.'

That was an extremely rare case of wishful thinking on Sir Alex's part. The couple had not fully settled in Cheshire – their main home was 200 miles away. And Victoria later admitted that she had been known to suggest to David that she'd be happier if he moved to a club down south. But at the time, everyone was keen to make and keep the peace – to a certain extent. It later emerged that the club fined David £50,000 as a penalty for his unauthorised night out – and, ironically enough, it was David's fashion sense that had given the game away. He attracted even more notice than usual because he was wearing a bandanna on his head – and so attracted Sir Alex's notice by appearing in all the papers.

But David let nothing come in the way of being a

family man. He began to take Brooklyn to training – and, according to Victoria, he would even make her a packed lunch before setting off for the day. The couple also got rid of their Rottweilers, according to some reports, fearing that the dogs might become jealous of Brooklyn. Brooklyn was indeed causing the couple some concern: in December, Victoria lunged at a man who seemed to be making threatening gestures as she and David left Harrods – David, of course, was holding the baby.

And Victoria continued to make controversial comments about her husband. As the year drew to an end, she accused United of underpaying him, pointing out that United captain Roy Keane was earning £50,000 – twice as much as David. Asked if she'd told him to approach Sir Alex, she replied, 'Certainly! Wouldn't you? I would love to say no but that would be lying.' Pouring oil on the flames, she continued that she wanted him to move abroad. 'I don't want to sound too shallow, but it's got to be somewhere a bit hot,' she continued. 'I don't want anywhere too grim. Italy, Spain, somewhere like that, I imagine. I think sometime in the future David would want to go abroad.'

She was right. But that time was still some way ahead. For now, David was quite simply a national hero.

Chapter Ten

Millennium Man

By the start of the new millennium, David's fame had grown so great that he was now the subject of security scares. United were due to fly to Brazil in early January to play in the World Club Championships and there were real fears that they might be the subject of a kidnapping attempt. In total, the club's players were worth at least £100 million, with David alone accounting for £30 million of that. The Brazilians were ordered to step up security. 'We have done everything we can to minimise the risk to the team,' said Rio police chief Major Marinho. 'We don't expect problems, but there is always the possibility of one.'

The team headed for Rio, with an anxious Victoria telling David to be careful. She had also repeated her comment in an interview to the effect that David wore her underpants, resulting in a further flurry of newspaper headlines. David had other things to worry about: in the opening game of the World Club Championship in Rio he was sent off during the team's first game against the Mexican side Necaxa. Fergie – who had also been told to leave the 'technical area' following a row with a FIFA official – was supportive. 'The Mexican players got David sent off,' he said, while dismissing his own contretemps – and the match ended in a 1–1 draw.

All of that was completely overshadowed when a Sunday newspaper ran a story claiming that there was indeed a kidnap plot – but it involved Victoria and Brooklyn, not David. Although it later turned out that the paper had paid £10,000 for a story without much foundation, it caused serious alarm, and the couple immediately arranged for increased security at all times.

The circus surrounding the family just continued to grow. Kevin Keegan, the then England manager, attempted to defuse some of the pressure when he said, 'To me, David Beckham is not a celebrity but a tremendously talented player – and that's all I'm interested in. In the back of my mind I know there are other things that come with him, with Michael Owen and with Alan Shearer. But they're not celebrities when they're with England. The problem people like David face is that everybody is trying to get a piece of the action because the media is a monster, which needs feeding constantly.

'But I've never seen any indication that the pressure is getting to David. He mixes well with all the boys. Whenever he comes in to the England squad he's a model player, and I've never had any problems with him. He's a winner and it goes without saying he's a tremendous player. The judgement on David now, though, is either a positive or a negative – there's nothing in between. He's either at the top of the sky or down in the pits, but as a manager I try to go along a middle line.'

United were certainly only too keen to hang on to David at that time. His pay was inching ever higher, now at around the £60,000-a-week mark as the club sought to fend off interested rivals. And it was David's father, of all people, who hinted that, if the couple continued to be on the receiving end of unkind treatment, then they might pack up and go abroad. 'What has been going on is an absolute disgrace,' he said. 'I know how high profile David is, but there is more serious news going on than my lad being splashed all over the front pages. I think it is a shame because he's just a footballer, after all, and the media are trying to make him into something he isn't. He won't want to leave England but anything is possible at the end of the day.' When the day finally came, of course, it was not the media who pushed David abroad. But at that stage no one dreamed of the rift that was to develop between David and Sir Alex.

David responded to this in typical fashion: he put on his bandanna and went out to face the photographers. Victoria, meanwhile, went on TV chat show *Parkinson*, where she tackled the ongoing speculation as to whether David wore her knickers or not. 'It was a joke. I mean, as if he'd wear my knickers, come on,' she said.

But the damage was done. It had just given rivals fans yet another stick with which to beat poor Becks.

They certainly couldn't taunt him with his performance on the field, though. At the end of January, United beat Middlesborough 1–0, with David scoring a goal in the 88th minute, his first of the Premiership season. Football commentators were forecasting that his game could only get better: it was a much-needed boost after the public-relations fiasco in Rio.

And still his profile continued to rise. It seemed that hardly a day could go by without David making the news and, indeed, the latest news about the boy was that he now had a stalker. She'd taken to visiting the couple's Cheshire home and leaving love letters and gifts – including her knickers. The letters included one saying, 'Sex is strong – so believe in it!' Another read, 'Situation 69 is blowing my mind!'

This was not long after the kidnap threat to Victoria, and Beckham took no chances: he contacted the police. They, in turn, discovered that his stalker was a 14-stone, 36-year-old former escort girl called Chinyelu Obue. She, in turn, seemed a little bewildered by the fuss. 'I now know I've got no chance with him,' she said, after being warned off by the police. I'm usually 13? to 14 stone. I suppose that's a little different from what he's used to with Victoria. I've got my own sex appeal and plenty of admirers, but I admit I once wanted to sleep with David. Some stuff I wrote was a bit porno. I never wanted to hurt him. I just wanted to make him smile.'

He needed a smile. Given the intensification of media interest since his marriage to Victoria, David was again under the eagle eye of Sir Alex, and Sir Alex didn't like what he saw. The two were involved in a furious row during training in February, when the United manager accused David of spending time in London the previous day when he should have been training. The row got so intense that David finally threw his gloves away and stormed off United's new training ground in Carrington. He was later seen driving away in his black Range Rover, again fuelling speculation that he might be prepared to leave the club.

And, indeed, the situation promptly got worse. It emerged that David's absence had been caused by a health scare involving Brooklyn. The 11-month-old boy became ill during the night, prompting Victoria to phone a doctor at 3am. The doctor diagnosed gastroenteritis. Wanting to stay home and care for his son, David phoned in to say he couldn't make training.

'Brooklyn was coughing and being sick in the middle of the night, and they called the doctor because they didn't know what was wrong with him,' said a spokesman for the couple. 'They were very worried. Obviously David wanted to stay with his son.'

But it was not obvious to Sir Alex. In his eyes this was not the way a footballer should behave and the sin was compounded by the fact that David was in Hertfordshire, not Cheshire. One row was nowhere near enough to clear the air: David was dropped from the forthcoming match against Leeds United and, not even picked for the substitutes' bench, was forced to watch the match from the stands.

'I picked the team for today and that's it,' said Sir Alex. 'In this situation I didn't pick David. What happened is just one of those things. What we do is inside the club and all things will be dealt with by the club.'

It didn't help that Victoria had been photographed at the British Fashion Awards ceremony on the night that David missed training, albeit without her spouse in tow. But it was the first really serious clash between player and manager since the wedding and many took it to be a sign of the increasing hold Victoria had over her husband. It was also the start of real tensions between the formidable Victoria and Sir Alex. The latter had never much cared for Victoria's world but now they had entered into a battle with one another for David's heart and soul and, right from the start, it was obvious who was going to win – Victoria. But when that finally happened, David would have to go.

Kevin Keegan stepped in to play peacemaker. He picked David to play midfield against Argentina – and no one missed the significance of that – when England played in a friendly. 'What happened at Leeds is a Manchester United thing and only two people can sort that out,' he said. 'It saddens Alex Ferguson, it saddens David Beckham and it saddens me. But sometimes manager and players have fallouts and you have to be realistic about that. But as far as I am concerned, David is fit and raring to go, as enthusiastic as ever, and was the last one off the training field as usual.

'On Wednesday, David can again show people what he can do with a football. He might benefit from the chance to return from this setback in style because he has an awful lot going for him as a player and a person. I know some people have concerns but I am not worried about his temperament and I never have been. He will be champing at the bit to play and will find a way of doing the job I ask of him as he always does.

'I put my trust in him because to me he's just a footballer. People talk about the other things going on in his life and they underestimate him because they don't know him. People pick up the bits and build an image, which I don't think is the guy. Having talked with him, trained with him, worked with him, I don't share those opinions. I see a very determined character who loves playing football and those are the qualities you need at the top. I would not give him responsibility if I didn't think he had the talent or the temperament to handle it. This match will be the sort of challenge he will relish.' And indeed he did. The game ended in a 0–0 draw, but Beckham put in a good performance and for now, at least, the ructions died down.

David's love of his high-profile lifestyle, however, continued to grow. He and Victoria did a photo session with Annie Leibovitz, one of the world's top photographers, to be published in *Vanity Fair*. The two were pictured rolling around each other at the Cawdor Estates, Inverness, ending with a shot of Victoria straddling her husband as he lay on a pool table. The pictures were stunning – and did nothing to stop David's growing celebrity.

Nor did the couple hold back when it came to Brooklyn's first birthday party. They laid on a £10,000 bash at Cotton's Hotel in Knutsford, Cheshire, inviting 100 guests along for the party. The theme was a circus, with no less than four clowns in attendance to amuse the assembled crowd. The children got burgers and the adults munched on lobster as little Brooklyn, dressed in a maroon bomber jacket with cream leather sleeves, held court. Guests included Gary Neville, with brother Phil and his wife Julie, Paul Scholes with wife and baby, Denis Irwin plus his three children and many more. Some adults, including Ryan Giggs and Mark Bosnich, turned up later. It was a resounding success.

'We have got him lots of toys,' said Victoria on her way in. 'It all looks fantastic in there.'

'It was a massive production,' said a member of the hotel's staff. 'Just converting the room at the back of the hotel into the way they wanted it took quite some time and plenty of effort. But there was plenty of laughter coming from the room. Brooklyn's parents really pushed the boat out and everyone obviously enjoyed the party.'

It also marked the end of the row between David and Sir Alex – for now, at least. David spoke publicly about the spat. 'It disappoints me that a little argument between me and the manager was blown up out of all proportion,' he said. 'I felt I had a good reason to miss training. Brooklyn was ill with gastro-enteritis. I rang the club and told them that. In the end I abided by what the manager and the club decided and accepted their disciplinary action. I have heard it said I'm trying to be bigger than the club. I'm not and never could be. Nobody can be bigger than the biggest club in the world.

'My relationship with the manager is fine. Players sometimes have bust-ups with their managers but it doesn't mean they have to fall out permanently. With our manager, you can have an argument with him one day and it will be forgotten the next. He's had his say and I've had mine. He's never mentioned it to me since and he doesn't bear grudges.'

Ferguson confirmed that it was all in the past. 'The players know I don't hold grudges,' he said. 'I haven't got the time to hold a grudge. I just want to get on with the game. That applies to all the players and David is no different from anyone else. I have had a chat with David. All we can say about him now is that the matter is cleared. It's over. It was finished on the day it began. I hope David is now saying the same positive things about the situation.'

He certainly was. Keen to ensure his loyalty to the club and smooth over any tensions between his wife and his manager, David could scarcely have been more positive. 'I love Manchester United with a passion,' he said. 'It's the only club I ever wanted to play for and I still do. Victoria doesn't want anything to affect that. She has never had a fallout with the manager. She respects him. People are trying to create a rift between them, but I can tell you, it doesn't exist.'

If that were not enough, David went on to talk about Victoria's feelings about Manchester. 'It's annoying that so many people seem to believe that Victoria hates Manchester and living up here,' he said. 'She spends much of her time in Manchester. The only time she's in London is when she's working. People seem to have this idea that I commute to work between London and Manchester every day. It's nonsense. We have an apartment in Alderley Edge and that is our home. It's where Victoria, Brooklyn and I live. We've bought a house down south and we'll probably live there eventually because that's where we both come from. But that is way in the future.' The message could not have been clearer. Everything in the garden was rosy and David had absolutely no intention of leaving Man U.

Despite the sudden outbreak of peace, though, David had no intention of adopting a lower profile. And so it was that startled fans saw a sharply crew-cut David run out on to the pitch when United played Leicester, having spent £300 having his locks trimmed. Any bemusement Sir Alex might have felt – and he almost certainly did – would have been allayed by the outcome of the match at least: United won 2–0, with one of the goals scored by Beckham. To celebrate, Brooklyn was given a similar cut.

Trivial as it was, David's haircut made both the front pages and the comment pages of the papers, with speculation rife about why he'd done it – to look more manly, said some, who clearly knew nothing about David's blithe disregard for his detractors – and whether he would lose his Brylcreem sponsorship. It was extraordinary that a man, and a footballer, to boot, should attract such attention merely over his appearance, but the public simply could not get enough of Posh and Becks. Every move the two of them made was reported on and every time they changed their partings there was saturation coverage. There was also a rumour that someone had been combing through the hair salon's rubbish bins to get their hands on David's shorn locks.

It is often asked why the two have such an appeal

but the answer is simple: they are young, beautiful, rich and in love. They are Prince Charles and Princess Diana, except with a happy ending. They have a lifestyle that most people can only dream about and on top of that their devotion to one another is genuine. Who wouldn't want to be Posh or Becks? Who wouldn't want to look that good themselves, have that good-looking a spouse, have such a successful career and to be feted wherever they went? It's no surprise David and Victoria enjoy their lifestyle – who wouldn't?

Of course, the one worry was Brooklyn and David acknowledged that. 'Fatherhood has changed me,' he said. 'I look at life from a different perspective. It's the best feeling and has made the relationship between me and Victoria even stronger. We'd like three or four kids but not yet. We want to enjoy watching Brooklyn grow up. We get worried for him because of all the attention we attract, which is why we have security with us at all times. But we try to act as normal as possible. We're doing our best.'

He was also keen to deny rumours to the effect that Victoria dominated him. 'She's always being asked who wears the trousers in the relationship,' he said. 'I can assure you, I'm my own man, but we make the big decisions about our life together. What some people don't realise is that Victoria says a lot of things tongue-in-cheek. The comment about me wearing her knickers was a joke. Everyone should have known that. But for four or five days it was all people wanted to talk about. It was embarrassing and she shouldn't have said it – even in jest. But then we had a laugh about it. It didn't cause any problems between us.'

David was also feeling sensitive about his reputation as a party animal. 'All people want to talk about is this person who wears sarongs and bandannas,' he grumbled. 'That annoys me. It seems to have been forgotten that I've spent most of my life working hard to earn a place in one of the top sides in the world. Some people are trying to turn me into a bad boy, which I never have been and never will be. I've never been pictured with a beer in my hand staggering all over the place. Occasionally we go to eat out at The Ivy, where you find a lot of celebrities. But we don't go there to be flash. When we visit some places we can't eat because people are coming up continually to ask for autographs. In The Ivy they don't let anyone ask for autographs. I know this because Michael Jordan was in there one night and I wasn't able to get his signature!'

David was, indeed, working hard, as were the rest of the team. United continued to go from strength to strength, receiving the Premier League Trophy in May. David shaved his head especially for the occasion and took Brooklyn on to the pitch. Roy Keane and Raymond van der Gouw also brought their own offspring on to the field, while Sir Alex cradled his grandson Jake.

As summer approached, David got his next tattoo: a figure of an angel looking down on the Brooklyn tattoo. Then a group of fans went one step further and decided that Beckham, too, should be a figure of worship. The fans, who lived in Thailand, made a 12-inch-high, gold-leafed statue of Becks, which they placed in the inner sanctum of the Pariwas temple in Bangkok. The monks didn't seem to mind. 'If it brings people to the temple, it will have done some good,' said one.

With Euro 2000 on the cards, attention finally turned back to the football field and playing for England. Kevin Keegan again voiced his support for the young star. 'Beckham can have a bigger influence on the England set-up than he has had already,' he said. 'I'm not scared to tell him because he knows that as well. There is no limit to how good he can become. He is still young, yet very experienced. Whatever he wants to be, he can be. There's so much more in him.'

Keegan was not alone in that opinion. Brazil ace Roberto Carlos told his teammates that the best way to ensure a victory is this: stop Beckham. 'Beckham is England's main player,' he said. 'Every time they have the ball, they look to get it to him. If he gets time and space to cross he will cause any team in the world problems.' There can be no higher praise than words such as this from a man you are to meet on the pitch. He was even voted second-best footballer in the world after Rivaldo.

David and Victoria took a short break in the States with Brooklyn before David reappeared, looking refreshed and ready for the trials ahead. Everyone was forecasting that he could be the best footballer in the world and now he seemed determined to make it happen. 'I've never felt better in my life,' he said. 'I've got bags of confidence right now. I've come off a good season, won another trophy and I've started to score goals. Now I want to dominate games for England more than I do. I really feel ready.'

And so Euro 2000 kicked off, with England playing Ukraine. Much to David's dismay, however, he again had to put up with abuse from the fans – many of them England fans who had still not forgotten the match against Argentina in 1998. David made a public plea for them to stop hating him and stand behind him, prompting words of comfort from a surprising quarter – Rivaldo.

'I have always had big pressure on me, it's nothing new – but since I was declared the best player there are new pressures,' he said. 'Although I know there are always people looking at what I do and how I play, I'm very calm and serene and try to do my job on the field. I keep working as hard as I've always done and I don't give too much significance to the pressure. When the game starts, I forget everything people tell me, everything people say about me, all the advice that newspapers or TV give me. I try to play my game with tranquillity and I think I am successful in doing that.

'That's the best way for Beckham to deal with things, just switch off. I believe this is the way to cope with pressures. Each player has different ways of coping with it and I don't know what his personality is. And, in Beckham's case, there are different matters that may affect his performance because he has a very famous wife. People see him in a different light because of that and the pressure goes beyond the football pitch. But I can't really give him any advice because he knows what to do on the field and he should know his ways of handling it.'

Euro 2000 did not start well for England. The team lost 3–2 to Portugal, although David himself played brilliantly. When he went to acknowledge the fans, however, he received such a volley of abuse that he ended up giving them a one-fingered gesture. As with Leeds, no one blamed him. The fans concerned were a disgrace to their country and the match: they chanted threats against Brooklyn, before turning their putrid little minds to Victoria and calling her a whore.

Kevin Keegan was staunchly supportive. 'I'd have thumped them,' he declared angrily. 'It was the worst thing I've seen in football. I've taken plenty of abuse in my time but this was way beyond anything I've heard. It was very personal. If you'd heard that abuse, if your sons and daughters had to listen to that, you'd have reacted in the same way.'

The entire nation felt the way Keegan did and rallied to David's defence. David responded brilliantly and went on the attack: the second game went far better, with England beating Germany 1–0. This time round he walked off the field to cheering, partly in recompense for treatment he had received previously. And when, a few days later, England lost 3–2 to Romania and crashed out of Euro 2000, David, in particular, was given thunderous applause as he left the field.

It was a momentous occasion in more ways than one because, for the first time, speculation began to mount that David might captain England. Alan Shearer was retiring and, although Keegan had been talking of Tony Adams as his replacement, Adams had not played as well as Beckham in the previous matches and was no longer considered a sure thing.

Shearer himself called on Keegan to hand David the prize. 'I have a great deal of pride when I pull on an England shirt but to captain my country would be the ultimate dream for me,' said Beckham. 'I have always harboured dreams of captaining the teams I play for, be they Manchester United or England, and I can think of no greater honour.'

The weeks after Euro 2000 gave David some time with his family. Victoria was working hard to promote her first solo single, a collaboration with True Steppers and Dane Bowers called 'Out Of Your Mind', and David dutifully accompanied her on a series of appearances, including an appearance at Party In The Park. Loyal as ever, he stood in the front of the crowd videoing her – she was later criticised for miming – before giving her a big hug when she came off the stage. The couple proceeded to tour England to publicise the record, including a much-discussed appearance at Woolworth's in Oldham. David came in for criticism for trooping around after Victoria and Victoria came in for criticism for dragging him around after her but, as ever, the couple blithely ignored the sniping and got on with their jobs.

But, while David might have been taking a rest from football, football was not taking a rest from him. Despite England's overall performance in Euro 2000, he had emerged with credit and was again being wooed by various rival clubs. This time around AC Milan had him in their sights and had approached Sir Alex to ask if he was for sale: the answer was no. At that time Sir Alex wouldn't hear of it and his decision was final.

David, Victoria and Brooklyn headed off for a quick break in the South of France, where they stayed first in the St Tropez villa of Harrods owner Mohamed Al Fayed and then at Sir Elton John's place near Nice. During their time at St Tropez, the couple were invited on to Fayed's yacht *Sakara*. 'David and Victoria looked really pleased to be invited on board,' said a friend. 'They were spotted joking and laughing with Mr Al Fayed as they all downed champagne in the sun. Posh and Becks got to know Mr Al Fayed through their frequent trips to his Harrods store. He had told them that his villa was always available if they wanted it.'

But then, to everyone's surprise, Sir Alex risked

reopening old wounds on the publication of an updated version of his autobiography. He had written about the furious argument he'd had with David earlier in the year, which led to him dropping Beckham for the match with Leeds. 'It doesn't matter to me how high a player's profile is,' he wrote. 'If he is in the wrong, he is disciplined. And David was definitely in the wrong.' It emerged he was particularly angry that Victoria had ventured out while David stayed at home. 'I had to think that David wasn't being fair to his teammates,' he went on. 'I had to imagine how they would feel if David could adjust the schedule to suit himself. There was no way I could consider including Beckham in the team to meet Leeds. That much was crystal clear in my mind before David worsened the problems between us when we met on the Saturday by making me lose my temper badly, something I hadn't done in years. At first he simply refused to accept he had anything to answer for and that made me blow up.'

One result of that, at least, was to bring out the predators from rival teams who still wanted to get their hands on David. 'I note with interest that Sir Alex Ferguson and David Beckham seem to have a difference of opinion that has not gone away,' commented Joan Gaspart, the newly elected president of Barcelona. AC Milan, having tried at least twice that summer to buy David, also pricked up its ears.

Martin Edwards, chairman of United, stepped in to quash rumours about both David and his teammate

Paul Scholes. 'There is no way we would allow them to go,' he snapped. 'They are the backbone of this team and we want them to remain at United. We would be extremely reluctant to see either player leave.'

David maintained a diplomatic silence. He could afford to. Just for once it seemed that Fergie was unwise, to put it mildly, to bring up that row again, especially after both had gone to such lengths to publicly avow it was all over. Fergie himself felt vindicated as far as the row itself was concerned, as it made David spend more time in Cheshire. But once more it had highlighted David's new-man qualities, his willingness to step away from the traditional image of a footballer and his love of his family. And now he was about to stun everyone yet again when he publicly welcomed his new role – that of gay icon.

David Beckham after the final whistle for Man U vs. Madrid in the UEFA
Champions League.

Top: Another goal for Beckham; this time against Finland.

Bottom: Becks receives the captain's armband form coach Peter Taylor.

Top left: The evening after being named top sports star in the fashion stakes at the Elle Style Awards, 1999. David steps out with Posh Spice in the sarong that whipped the tabloids into a frenzy. Nowadays, Beckham's numerous hairstyle changes never fail to make the front pages.

Top right: The happy couple out walking their puppy Rottweilers.

Bottom: Engaged!

Top left: Already the perfect family, Victoria, David and Brooklyn leave Victoria's mum's house to go to the airport. They flew to Ireland for their wedding.

Top right: And what a wedding it was! 14½ months in the planning, the union of Posh and Becks overshadowed even that of Prince Edward and Sophie Rhys-Jones.

Bottom left: The man who made fatherhood sexy. David shops with Brooklyn … again.

Bottom right: David's football boots – the name of the newly born 'Romeo' has been added above his brother's.

Top: David Beckham has been adored – but also despised. The picture shows Arsenal fans watching an Arsenal Vs Man U match during the Charity Shield.

Bottom left: That red card – Becks is sent off by referee Kim Milton Nielson during the second round match between Argentina vs England in the World Cup Finals, 1998.

Bottom right: A dummy hanging as a representation of David Beckham. This was the work of south London football hooligans after the England vs Argentina match in the 1998 World Cup.

With all the pressures of intensive media coverage on top of his football career, David needs all the relaxation he can get. *Top*: David is pictured on holiday in Marbella, kissing a pregnant Victoria. *Bottom*: The couple's huge mansion in the south of England, dubbed 'Beckingham Palace' by the press.

Top left: The fame of David Beckham has spread well into the East. This golden statue of the footballer has been placed at the foot of the main Buddha image in Bangkok's Pariwas Temple together with a hundred or so other minor deities.

Top right: David Beckham out shopping with a very visible wound above the eye where he was hit and cut by a flying boot kicked by Sir Alex Ferguson. The whole nation read it as a grim sign of their disintegrating relationship.

Bottom: A very shiny couple present a prize during the 2003 MTV Movie awards. David was to find out about his sudden change of fate during this profile-raising trip to the States.

A golden future for 'Goldenballs'? Beyond doubt is that Man United's loss is Real Madrid's gain.

Chapter Eleven

Glad to Be – Eh?

And so, David, asked the interviewer brightly, how does it feel to be a gay icon? No one who knew David would have been surprised by the answer. 'Actually, I think it's cool,' he said. 'Other people may have a problem with it, but whether men or women fancy you, it's always nice to be liked. I think it's great.'

It went on. When did David first become aware of the attention from gay men? 'I was getting mentions in magazines like *Attitude* as soon as I started playing for Manchester United,' said David. 'Obviously you get a bit of stick from other footballers about things like that because football is supposed to be such a macho game. There's that attitude of "I'm a footballer, I go down the pub, drink beer." But I've never been that type of person. I prefer to go to a nice restaurant or bar with my wife. That's my perfect night out.'

Had David ever been sucked into that kind of laddishness? 'No not at all,' he said. 'Of course, I've tried it – I've gone out and tried drinking loads, eating an Indian and throwing up but it didn't suit me. Not as a person and certainly not as a husband.'

David was then asked if he'd ever been chatted up by gay men. 'Yes, a couple of times,' said David cheerfully. 'We go to gay bars – not every week, but quite a bit, so I get a bit of that. I've had wolf whistles from blokes as well. It doesn't bother me and Victoria thinks it's cool.'

Victoria herself revealed how much her husband revelled in his new-found status. 'He's a big flirt and he loves it,' she said to DJ Jeremy Joseph on his *G-A-Y* show on radio station Spectrum. 'He walks around the kitchen saying, "I'm a gay icon, I'm a gay icon", and when I try to say, "So am I," he just goes, "But they love me, you've got nothing on me, baby."'

It is a rare man, let alone footballer, who could have come out with that, but it was typical of David. For the fact is that he is so secure in his own sexuality – and he and Victoria have a very passionate love life as in that same interview she talked about him being an animal in bed – that he is able to accept compliments from both sexes without batting an eyelid. It is the same quality that allows him to wander around in sarongs, wear nail varnish and have his wife go on television in Japan to tell the world that he likes facials. David simply doesn't care what other people think. He minds when he gets hatred on the football pitch, as would anyone, but, off the pitch, he goes his own way.

Very rarely, David goes too far and has to be hauled back for his own good. A case in point was at that time: David was sporting a skinhead look but what he had really wanted was to have a Mohican haircut. Sir Alex put his foot down and made David shave it off. 'I couldn't have it, which I was gutted about because it looked wicked,' David said sadly. 'But the manager didn't think I needed the publicity or a slaughtering in the papers for the next week.

'I watched the film [*Taxi Driver*] the other night and thought, That's wicked, so I got Tyler [David's hairdresser] round to do it. We were in the changing room before the game and he [Sir Alex] turned to me and asked, "Are you going to shave it off?" To be fair, he wasn't nasty about it – he just said I didn't need the abuse – and at the end of the day I don't. He was only really looking out for my best interests, I think. I suppose in a way I wanted to keep it and I would have if he hadn't said anything. But he's the boss and sometimes you've got to listen to him. Well, *most* of the time.'

David's maturity, noticeable even when he was a teenager, would have led to his inner security whatever way his life had gone, but his marriage to

Victoria only served to heighten it. The couple's closeness and devotion to each other is not, alas, to be found in many relationships and he knew it. 'Our relationship is the sort that most people don't have and one I think most people would love to have,' David said simply. 'I think people like to see the way we act!

'It's not just a thing we do in front of the cameras. We go out, we hold hands. We're always holding hands, you know – whatever. Even if it's watching a film we're always holding hands or cuddling. That's the way we've always been and, in a lot of ways, I think people like to see that – it's that fairytale thing. Maybe we'll get slaughtered for it but it's not for show, it's for real. We love each other so much it hurts. It's at that stage where we don't do things for publicity, we do it because we're like that at home. We're like that when we're watching telly. We do it all the time.'

David was absolutely right. He had summed up exactly why the public are so interested in the two of them. An ancient Greek philosopher once said that, when human beings first peopled the world, they had four arms, four legs and cartwheeled around in a state of bliss. But the gods were jealous of their happiness and so split them in half and ever since then humans have been destined to wander the world, searching for that lost other half. Some find it, some don't. David and Victoria did.

But David's closeness to Victoria meant it was

inevitable he would take a step back from his parents. 'I was definitely a mummy and daddy's boy for a long, long time,' said David. 'I was dependent on my mum and dad in all ways, whereas I think later I learned other things and grew up. Since I've met Victoria, I've done that a lot. I've not been as dependent on my mum and dad, and whoever else I depended on in the past. I love my mum and dad and they're always going to be there for me. But it's the same with them, I'm sure. At a point in their lives, they turned round and needed each other more than their own mums and dads. But you always need your mum and dad, whatever.'

David is also far more intelligent than he is usually given credit for. His misfortune is his voice: it is soft and whispery rather than deep and resonant and so tends to belie his actual words. But, if you read what David is saying rather than listen to him, it's clear that he has an inner maturity and intelligence that a great many people do not possess. Apart from anything else, you do not achieve the fame and riches that David has without some sort of inner quality and, if, say, he had a voice like Stephen Fry, he would come across as witty and self-deprecating rather than a bit 'not all there'. But, being David, even this failed to bother him.

As the new football season approached, there was a noticeable change in the fans' attitude. There was a sense that they had gone too far during Euro 2000 and almost seemed to be trying to make it up to him. At a pre-season match in York, the fans actually cheered him as he ran out on to the pitch, much to David's own bemusement. 'It was nice to get a good reception at York,' he said. 'In pre-season last year I was getting booed here and there, but it made a nice change at the weekend.'

David's new-found popularity went straight to his pocket. Well aware that rival clubs would grab him the moment they could, it was rumoured that United offered to raise David's pay packet to £80,000 a week. 'David will be here for as long as I'm manager,' said Ferguson. 'He's not pushing for any new negotiations on his contract and he's looking forward to the new season.' But he did hint that there might be a pay rise at the end of the season.

Kevin Keegan helped matters further when he hinted that David could become England captain. Autumn was turning into a gruelling time for Beckham – Victoria was upset when her single only got to Number 2 and she then went on to contract meningitis while touring in Europe. David had to cope with all that on top of his footballing career, but he carried on as normal, impressing the England manager with his coolness and determination. 'I would definitely say that one day David could captain England, but there are processes to go through,' he said. 'He might not be the most vocal of players but he's got leadership qualities.'

Jackie Adams moved Victoria and Brooklyn to Goff's Oak, so David could fly to Paris with the England squad for a friendly game against France, followed by the European and World Championships.

There were the usual rumours about the possibility of his moving abroad, the usual round of denials from everyone and then, in October, the publication of *Beckham: My World*, a sort of coffee-table volume full of pictures of, well, David. It also contained a few telling insights about his life. David revealed that he would love to go skiing when he eventually stops playing football as he can't currently do so because of the insurance, and that he would love to fly to the moon one day, were it ever possible.

He also talked about building a football pitch at the new home in Hertfordshire and having horses. 'The new house is perfect for a five-a-side pitch for me and Brooklyn,' he wrote. 'I'd like us to have three or four more babies. That would keep me busy.' And there was every chance that they would do so, given that he went on to write, 'I'm often asked whether scoring a goal is better than sex. For me there is no contest. Of course, sex is better.'

And, of course, the book was a best-seller. As the hostility created by the 1998 match against Argentina died away, it was replaced by straightforward hero worship. David turned up at Manchester's Trafford Centre for a book signing, where he was mobbed by a crowd of thousands; it included teenage girls crying, 'I'd die for you, David,' and parents lifting their children above the heads of the crowd to get a glimpse of the great man. 'It's mad,' said one of the security guards present. 'There's been nothing like this since the Irish singer Daniel O'Donnell was here.'

With all of this adulation going on and a book to publicise, it was almost inevitable that David would end up on *Parkinson*. Wearing a black suit and a pair of sparkling diamond earrings, he took the opportunity to address some of the more telling issues of the day. 'I can actually say I have not worn Victoria's knickers – not in public, anyway,' he said. 'It will be a bit worrying if I did because she is smaller than me. When Victoria starts talking, sometimes she can't stop. She says things that get a bit of coverage but I love her still, so it doesn't matter.'

Victoria was there, hidden in the wings with Brooklyn, while about 30 of David's family and friends, including his parents, sisters and parents-in-law were in the audience to give David a bit of confidence. 'David was in knots about appearing on the show,' said a friend. 'He wanted to look out there and see as many friendly faces in the audience as possible.'

There was also something different about his voice. Onlookers thought he might have taken elocution lessons to deepen it slightly.

Rather ironically, given what was to happen, David also said that he did not feel the need to move abroad to become the best possible player. 'I don't believe that to reach my coming of age as a player I would have to move to the Italian or Spanish leagues,' he said. 'A lot of people say that you must move to Spain or Italy to become one of the best, or to prove yourself, but I don't believe that. I feel that I will stay in England as long as my family are happy and I am happy. The moment that changes, I will look at my options. But, if I am playing good football and getting headlines on the back pages, then I am happy. The press likes to say that Victoria wears the trousers and makes the decisions. But, at the end of the day, if I do leave United, it will be my choice, not Victoria's. As a family man I have to look at what will be best for the family. It will not be Victoria who says, "You have got to leave Manchester United because I want better shops in Milan or whatever."'

David also talked about Euro 2000, explaining that he, too, had found it to be a turning point with regard to the fans. Asked about flicking his finger he said, 'My reaction could have been far worse. You would have had to be a saint not to be hurt by the things being said about my wife and son. Oddly enough, after that people came out and supported me. They knew I didn't deserve that kind of treatment. It had been happening to me for two years, yet some people didn't believe it until they heard it in the summer. I think it shocked them to realise what I'd had to put up with. I get abuse even when I'm walking down the street. People shout, "Beckham, you are a so-and-so." It is not very pleasant for me and my family.'

Victoria helped him to cope, not least by pointing out that the fans who scream abuse are almost certainly jealous of David and his life. He was, after all, living many a young man's dream: sporting superstar, extremely wealthy and with a collection of cars that included Ferraris and Range Rovers. 'Victoria has always said to me, "They are getting their aggression out on you and going home to probably a sad life,"' he revealed. 'She always turns around and says that, if you are ever at that point [of lashing out] just think about what you've got and what you are doing. These people would do anything to play for Man United and England. I've got to think of that straight away or I could do something.'

Beckham had matured to the extent that he was even able to look back on the worst time of his life, after the match against Argentina in 1998, and say he'd gained something from it. For a player who was fundamentally mature but who had a tendency to lash out, in many ways it was the making of him. David had to learn to curb his temper both on and off the pitch, while receiving a level of abuse that would have destroyed a lesser man. But that which does not destroy you makes you stronger – and David was now at a stage where he was even ready to captain England.

My World continued to sell well – embarrassingly so. David did a book signing in London with Victoria and Brooklyn in attendance (all the critics who thought Victoria shouldn't have dragged him around with her when her record was released should note it worked both ways) and 8,000 fans turned up to get their signed copy. Signed copies of Sir Alex

Ferguson's autobiography were also on display – and sold only 500. 'We get queues for all book signings by famous people, but the turnout for Beckham is certainly the biggest.'

A further insight into the couple's lifestyle came when Victoria gave an interview to *Q* magazine, in which she described him as an 'obsessive compulsive'. 'He's got that obsessive compulsive thing where everything has got to match,' she said. 'He's got it, like, ridiculously. If you open our fridge, it's all co-ordinated down either side. If there are three cans of Diet Coke he'd throw one away rather than having three because it's uneven.' Clearly the tidy teenager who had lived with Annie and Tommy Kay had grown even more fastidious in his habits over the years.

And, of course, the thorny subject of the knickers came up again. 'I do often say things I shouldn't, but that's my personality,' Victoria confessed. 'When I said the thing about him wearing my knickers ... I'd never say anything to purposely make it difficult for him. I have learned my lesson but, in interviews, I am quite an honest person. I've got a dry sense of humour and I say things and unfortunately most of the media don't have a sense of humour. As if he'd fit in my bloody underwear! I'm a size six.

'But he's a very strong personality, David. He would never do anything he didn't want to. People think he's some kind of idiot and Posh Spice says to him, "Oh, put on this skirt, David, it'll look really great." And then he goes out looking like a prat. He's really not like that. He's a good-looking bloke, he's got the body to wear whatever he wants to wear and look amazing in it. And he loves it. If he didn't love it, he wouldn't dress like that. It's nothing to do with me.'

In October another dream came true: David was named as England captain as England prepared to play Italy in Turin. 'This is one of the proudest moments in my footballing career,' he said. 'When I was a kid, I used to dream about leading England out.'

England coach Peter Taylor, in charge for just this match, was in no doubt that Beckham was the right man for the job. 'He deserves to be captain,' he said. 'He'll take the responsibility on board, he'll respond to it and I hope in the right way. He has matured greatly since the 1998 World Cup. He is a marvellous player and I think he will handle the responsibility of leading the team. He looks like he desperately wants to play for Manchester United and England, that he loves his football and I intended to give him the captaincy from the moment the FA asked me to take charge for this one-off game. All the other players respect David and I see no reason why he can't go on and captain England for many years to come.'

Victoria was equally delighted for her husband. 'I'm really proud of him,' she said. 'He has worked really hard and I know he will be a fantastic captain. I'm so glad he has been given this chance.'

It almost goes without saying that David took his

new responsibilities seriously. 'I won't stand up and give a speech but it's my job to go up to players and talk to them,' he said. 'I'm not used to doing that because I'm quite shy. It'll be hard for me but I've got to learn to do things like this and I'm sure I'll do it. It's exciting because everyone's talking about the new era – it's great for me to be captain and to lead the team out. I've been quieter than some of the other captains – I won't be shouting. But I can give different things to the team.'

David was also looking forward to playing in midfield. 'I've got to change my game and talk to other players but hopefully I'll be able to do that,' he said. 'I'm pleased I'm playing in the centre as a captain because it'll give me more of a chance to speak to players a bit more and keep the team going. I know everyone will give 110 per cent – but to get a good result over here is really hard. Victoria wanted to come but she's working, though I'm sure she'll watch it on the telly. But my mum and dad will be here – it's going to be a proud moment for them. My dad's always watched England games, so to see me leading the team out will be a special moment for him. Two years ago, if someone had turned round and told me that in two years I would be England captain, I would have said, "I don't think so." I've got a lot of respect for Kevin Keegan as a man and a manager. I've got a lot to thank him for.'

It was the fulfilment of a dream, but as yet it was unclear how long David would be England captain. It had just been announced that Sven-Göran Eriksson was to be the new England manager and his thoughts about the captaincy were as yet unknown. But, if David was worried, he chose not to show it. Instead he decided to have another tattoo – this time the name Victoria, spelled out in Arabic on the inside of his left arm.

'I tried it in Chinese the other night and drew some characters,' he said. 'It looked good and Victoria was impressed but I copied it off a Chinese menu so I probably had "fried rice, salt and pepper ribs and hot and sour soup" on my arm instead of "Victoria"! I've wanted a new tattoo for ages, but we agreed it would look a bit tacky if I just had "Victoria" in English. So I've finally gone for Arabic because it's quite arty and I wanted something different. This is what I do when I'm bored – new tattoos, new cars, new watches. I sound like a right sad git.'

The new tattoo coincided with the release of a documentary video, *The Real David Beckham*, and again, if you read what David says rather than listen to him, he comes across as clever and witty. Here he is on the way to film *Parkinson*: 'It's an honour to be invited on his show because he's a legend. Everyone tries to catch me out and most of the time I do get caught out. He'll probably throw in a couple of long words that I don't understand. I'll just have to combine the little words that he says before that and make something up.' If that speech had been delivered in a Stephen Fry-esque baritone, it would have come across as witty and self-deprecating. But once again, poor old David's voice let him down.

He also revealed that he knew Sir Alex was not totally delighted with his lifestyle. 'Alex Ferguson would like me to go straight home from training, but I think he realises that doesn't happen any more,' he said. 'I like doing photo shoots because you can order pizza and McDonald's.' David was pretty unique in that, too. There can't be many models who feast on fatty food when their picture's being taken.

He also referred to the row over missing training when Brooklyn was ill. 'A lot of players have learned over the years, if you get on the wrong side of Alex Ferguson, it's not nice,' he said.

Sir Alex himself had his say. 'What David has to control is the publicity machine from Victoria's side – it has been interfering with his life and you can't have that,' he said. 'You are a footballer, your wife's job is different to yours. There is nothing worse than when you pick up a paper and see, "Oh Christ, where is he now?" I think he's tried hard to make sure that's under control a bit. Since that little argument, there's been better dialogue.'

But not, of course, for long. David was prepared to rein in his new lifestyle to a certain extent, but he was growing increasingly used to the trappings of fame, and fame is addictive: once you've got it, you don't want to give it up.

But equally, David put his fame to good use. As

Christmas approached, the couple visited Christie Hospital in Manchester, where they spent an hour distributing presents to children. It was an extremely generous gesture.

'The youngsters were thrilled,' said a spokesman for the Youth Oncology Unit. 'It's something they will never forget. David and Victoria asked for the visit to be kept quiet. They didn't want any publicity, but they made everyone's Christmas.'

David remained popular elsewhere, too. The ever-hopeful Barcelona popped up again, offering David a deal worth £100,000 a week. Ryan Giggs, Andy Cole, Dwight Yorke and Jaap Stam were also seen as potential defectors to other clubs. Sir Alex wasn't having any of it. 'I would put my life on them staying, as long as we look after them,' he said. 'Nothing is certain in life, but I don't think they want to leave Old Trafford. The important thing is to be top of the league on 1 January. If we are, we will be delighted.'

Christmas approached – David was spotted buying sexy underwear for Victoria at the exclusive London shop Agent Provocateur – and the family spent it with Victoria's parents at Goff's Oak. David's present to Victoria was generous, to put it mildly – a £300,000 state-of-the-art recording studio in Beckingham Palace. David presented her with architects' plans and explained he was having it built so that he and Brooklyn could come in to listen, and so that Victoria wouldn't be kept in London so late at night. Victoria was in tears at the gift.

In the new year, negotiations began over a new contract, with David reportedly turning down an opening offer of £80,000 a week. Under Victoria's guidance, it was believed that David was determined not just to achieve pay parity with his teammates, but to be paid better than the rest of them. Not everyone was thrilled that Victoria was involved in negotiations, not least the former Nottingham Forest boss Brian Clough. 'I'm watching David Beckham with great interest these days,' he said. 'I think he's at a personal crossroads where his great talent and professionalism may collide with his lifestyle. Beckham is a highly talented player who plays for the team and Alex Ferguson has done a brilliant job with him. When necessary he has cracked down on him and Beckham has juggled all the social balls well.

'But what happens when Alex retires? Will the glamour of Milan and Madrid get to him? When you're young you can get away with all the whizzing around but it does catch up with you. He's a very fit lad now but, if he stops doing his stuff on match day, all that magazine and documentary trivia will rebound on him. He should sign a new, long contract with United, persuade his missus to have a few more bairns and get as much rest as he can. And, while he's at it, he should guide Posh in the direction of a singing coach, because she's nowhere near as good at her job as her husband is at his. I used to like my players to marry young, but I had no time for wives who interfered with the football – it was up to my players to control their wives. Alex Ferguson is just as old-fashioned as I am about that.'

In retrospect, reading those words, a clash between Beckham and Ferguson was inevitable. It wasn't just the differing personalities and lifestyles of the two men, it was a generational sea change. In Ferguson and Clough's young days, wives were wives who did what they were told to do. These days, relationships are more equal and, in the case of David and Victoria, exceptionally close. Telling Victoria to keep quiet and keep her nose out of it was as useful as telling water to run uphill. It just wasn't going to happen.

Clough was not the only one to voice reservations about the effect Victoria was having on her husband's career and David didn't like it. The two were highly protective of one another and quick to jump to the other's defence when they thought it was needed. So, just as Victoria spent hours telling people that David isn't thick, he was equally quick to jump on people who accused her of interfering.

'I do want to stay at Manchester United and it will be my decision and not Victoria's,' he said as speculation mounted that he was aiming to become Britain's first £100,000-a-week footballer. 'There has been a lot written about my contract talks. About how much I have been offered and when it will be decided.

I have not started my contract talks yet, but I will be doing that soon. And, if I can reach agreement with the club, it is where I want to stay. This is where I have grown up. People claim she has her ideas about me moving abroad and about leaving United. People make out she's trying to pull me away from the club. But she isn't. She never has done. She loves living in Manchester and she is happy here – she always has been. But I will make my decision when I start talks with the club. It is a family decision but, at the end of the day, it will be my decision.'

The message was clear: David could look after his own career and didn't need his wife to do it for him. Nor was Victoria being pushy. But, of course, they discussed every move the other made because they are blessed with a strong and close relationship that allows them to do that. And, on top of that, David wanted to stay at Manchester United. But for how long?

Chapter Twelve

Captain Becks

As Sven-Göran Eriksson moved in as the new England manager, speculation intensified as to whether he would keep David on as captain. Some of the other players had reservations, thinking that, at 25, David was still too young for the job. Eriksson went to Manchester to watch United play early in the year, but ironically David had been given a rest day and was attending a music awards ceremony in the South of France. He and Victoria sported matching black outfits with silver crucifixes for the night. Eriksson was unperturbed.

'I knew on Friday that David would not be playing but it doesn't matter because as a player I know him,' he said. 'And it doesn't surprise me that he is being rested. Manchester United want to win the Champions

League, the Premiership and the FA Cup, and it is impossible for one player to play in all 60 or 70 games. You have to do these things. Alex Ferguson told me a couple of seasons ago that things like this are one of the secrets of United's success.'

He was guarded, though, as to whether David would retain the role of captain. 'I don't know about that.

I will wait until I get all the players together,' he said. 'I haven't spoken to David yet or any of the players.'

The speculation did nothing to dent David's popularity. He signed another sponsorship deal, this time with Police sunglasses, worth £1 million, and promptly splashed out on a £185,000 Lamborghini Diablo GT, adding to an already extensive collection. (In later years Sir Elton John was heard to remark, 'I keep telling David, buy paintings, not cars.') He then returned to the football field, helping United to a 6–1 win against Arsenal, prompting more comment about being England's most gifted footballer.

Meanwhile, England's most gifted manager – Sir Alex – was preparing for retirement. It is a mark of quite how much relations deteriorated in just two years that his most vocal fan, and one who wished him to stay on, was none other than Beckham himself. 'It's impossible for anyone to try to influence Sir Alex, but I certainly want him to stay,' he said. 'You only have to look at his track record to know what he has done for Manchester United and what a loss he will be when he eventually quits. He has been the only boss I have played for since I signed for United when I was 16. It has been an absolute dream to work with the greatest manager we have ever seen in this country. I have only to look at my collection of medals and England caps to appreciate the part he has played in my career.'

It was a typically generous remark of David's and he was to have his wish fulfilled. Sir Alex did agree to stay on after all. Whether David later came to regret what he said is unlikely, but certainly, had Ferguson left when he originally intended to, David might well still be at United today.

Having established that he was staying at United for now, David and Victoria volunteered their services for something quite different – Comic Relief. The two proved conclusively that they did not take themselves too seriously and indeed had a very well-developed sense of humour when they agreed to be interviewed by Ali G. Ali G, a spoof character created by the comedian Sacha Baron Cohen, was then at the height of his popularity and it was a brave man (and woman) who would subject themselves to what proved to be a merciless grilling.

The introduction was a taste of what was to come: 'Every boy wants to be in his boots and every man wants to be in his missus. Big up for none other than Victoria and David Beckham!' Ali then kicked off by telling David, 'Now, just because it's Comic Relief doesn't mean you can speak in a silly voice,' before asking if he could sleep with Victoria. He then went on to ask David if he'd really wanted to go out with Emma Bunton, aka Baby Spice, before embarking on the most memorable exchange of the evening:

Ali G: 'So tell me, does Brooklyn like your music or is he getting a bit old for it now?'

Victoria: 'Well, yeah, he does like music, he jigs about and dances. He's also into football as well, so it's nice.'

Ali G: 'Respect, respect. So how old is Brooklyn now?'

Victoria: 'He's nearly two.'

Ali G: 'So tell me, is your little boy starting to put whole sentences together?'

Victoria: 'He's learning the bits and pieces, so yeah.'

Ali G: 'And what about Brooklyn?'

There followed barbed remarks about Victoria's weight, the future of the Spice Girls (who Ali managed to confuse with rival band All Saints) and the couple's taste in fashion, before an impassioned plea from Ali and the audience for David to strip off. 'Not even for charity,' he replied.

In all, the interview lasted 40 minutes, leaving both David and Victoria speechless at times. Afterwards the papers had a field day talking about how the two had been ridiculed, but in that they totally missed the point. The two would have known what talking to Ali G entailed and went ahead with it anyway, something many more self-important celebrities would have refused to do. In the same way, the two have admitted to laughing at the impersonations of them by Alistair McGowan and Ronni Ancona. David even once went so far as to say that they loved the sketch where David complained to Victoria that the peas were still in the pod, only to be told they were mangetouts. There aren't many people with the high profile of those two who would have been able to take the joke, but, say what you like about them, Victoria and David can. It is one of the many reasons that they can cope with their fame without going a little mad.

Shortly afterwards David played again as England captain and led the team to a 3–0 victory against Spain at Villa Park in Birmingham on his first outing under Eriksson at the end of February. Victoria, who could be seen wiping back tears, was in the crowd, holding Brooklyn.

'I was so proud of David because I know how much this means to him,' she said. 'It's the greatest honour to captain your country. When I saw him walking out with the armband leading his team as captain of England I was just completely overwhelmed and felt the tears welling up. It was really, really emotional and I had to try hard not to burst into tears. Holding Brooklyn as his dad walked out was one of the most amazing moments of my life. I was just completely filled with pride to see my husband and father of my baby leading the team.'

Of course, David was pleased, too, not least because the score gave the new England manager a very good reason for keeping him on as captain. He had been swapped at half-time, but the cool-as-ice Swede manager reassured everyone that that had been planned all along. 'The team performed well and I'm pleased, happy, proud of the performance. I know a little bit more now about the job and about the players. The spirit in the squad is very good and I'm feeling a bit warmer in the job now.'

To mark Brooklyn's second birthday, the Beckhams treated their son, United colleagues and their children to the freedom of a ball pool at a Wacky Warehouse fun pub. For the occasion, Brooklyn sported a tiny denim jacket with Chinese characters on it, almost identical to one worn by David. Champagne flowed for the adults and there was a birthday cake in the shape of a football pitch, while the children were entertained by clowns, stilt walkers, a magician and the Manchester United red devil. The couple were in fine form: they signed autographs for fans waiting outside, posed for pictures and even sent out some birthday cake. The fans loved it and sang 'Happy Birthday' to the little boy.

Slightly unsurprisingly, given this and his much-publicised adoration of his son, David was voted 'Perfect Dad' in a nationwide poll, beating Prime Minister Tony Blair, Bob Geldof, Fatboy Slim and

Michael Douglas. But David was feeling jaded. Sir Alex, expressing concern that David might be losing his form, gave him the weekend off, prompting the usual speculation that this might be the end of his time with United. David travelled down south to rest and look after Brooklyn, as Victoria was recording a new album, and also took the opportunity to do some shopping, buying a new four-wheel-drive BMW. He was also spotted having dinner with Victoria in The Ivy, wearing his favourite earrings: £20,000 diamond and platinum hoops from society jeweller Theo Fennell.

But, while he was resting from United, he was still playing for England and led the team out at Anfield, home of Liverpool, against Finland. This was another risky occasion: Liverpool fans were given to jeering at United players in general and Beckham in particular, leading Sven-Göran Eriksson to make a public plea for them to unite behind the team.

David was worried, not least because Victoria was also going to be there. 'Obviously I'm concerned about any stick my family might get,' he said. 'It would be nice for my wife to be able to go to the game and not worry about getting in or out of the ground. I love her coming to watch and I'm sure she'll be there. Hopefully, becoming England captain has eased it. Over the last year it has got a lot better. We understand we will get a certain amount of stick as players. The most important thing is we get on as professionals with winning the game.'

In the event, England won 2–1, with David scoring the deciding goal. It was a brilliant performance. Nervous about the reception she would get from fans, Victoria had been watching at the hotel with Brooklyn and was ecstatic. 'Brooklyn and I couldn't stop cheering when David scored. He's my hero and I love him,' said a breathless Mrs Beckham after the match. 'It was a great game. Brooklyn loved watching his dad and was shouting and pointing when the camera was on him. I was really nervous. I'd bought loads of crisps and drinks so we could watch it on the box, and we had our fingers crossed they'd win. David played brilliantly and his goal was even better. I got a bit emotional, I was so happy for him.'

The crowd was so delighted it sang, 'There's only one David Beckham' as he ran off, while teammates, including Steven Gerrard and Michael Owen, queued up to praise him. 'You look at David and he leads by example,' said Owen. 'It's important to have a captain who can perform like that.' More importantly still, it silenced the doubters who had wondered whether Eriksson was right to keep Beckham on as captain. His future now seemed assured.

David responded to all the rapture in typically modest style. 'I didn't hear the fans singing at the end,' he said. 'I was simply carried away in the moment, but to be told afterwards what they were chanting was just unbelievable. Brilliant. After getting off to a bad start we showed tremendous character to battle back, and when you do that I think any crowd will get behind you. I've never had to do so much talking on the pitch before. I'm not the kind of guy who goes around ranting and raving. My responsibility is to stay calm and talk to the younger players in particular. I can't believe I'm saying that. It makes me feel like an old man. But it's the captain's job to lead by example, whether he's a hard player or a player like me.'

And it meant all the more that the fans' singing had happened at Anfield. If Liverpool fans were finally prepared to cheer for David, then the events of 1998 really had been laid to rest. It also meant that Victoria would now be able to go to games to watch her husband without fear of abuse.

David's friend and teammate Gary Neville was also delighted and forecast that David would now captain England for some years to come. 'He's more assured and it's a necessity when you're made the England captain,' he said. 'All of a sudden you've got to take on more responsibility and it's not a problem for him. At 26 he's seen most things in football. There's not a lot that he's not seen: World Cups, European Championships, massive games for United. Sometimes at 25 or 26 you need that extra challenge, that extra motivation. Giving him the England captaincy will certainly have given him that and he can be England captain for years to come. Tony Adams and Alan Shearer retired and why not start afresh? The whole squad is a lot fresher, to be honest.'

It was a total, unqualified triumph for David, although he soon learned that, while Liverpool fans might cheer him on for England, it was a different story when he was playing for United. Just one week later he was back at Anfield and, while it was the first time he had played with United for some weeks now, it was not an auspicious occasion. The team lost 2–0, and taunts against Victoria were heard in the crowd. A week turned out to be a long time in football.

David was not unduly concerned: he had now officially attained the status of national hero. But tensions with his boss surfaced again after Sir Alex banned him from attending a charity awards ceremony in London with Victoria. He had been due to pick up the Sports Personality of the Year Award at the Capital FM Help A London Child appeal until Ferguson told him it was impossible to take time off at this stage of the season – despite the fact that he wasn't playing in the next two United matches.

He did, however, make it to London for Victoria's 27th birthday at the end of April a couple of weeks later. He was wearing sparkling white trainers for the event and when pictures were published Adidas, maker of the trainers, was swamped with requests for more pairs of the shoes. They were, however, specially made for David. And, while he didn't have to buy them himself, he could certainly afford to: in the newly published *Sunday Times* Rich List 2001, the Beckhams were said to be jointly worth £30 million. Victoria, incidentally, was still ahead of David, earning £18 million to his £12 million.

David was putting his money to good use where his wardrobe was concerned. Fashion pundits might sneer, but the fans loved it: he was voted Most Fashionable Footballer in the Premiership, easily beating the likes of Rio Ferdinand and David Ginola, in the Burton Menswear League of Football Style.

Beckham celebrated his 26th birthday in trademark style: he had a new hairdo, is time a close crop on top of the head and shaved on either side. It was known as a 'step' cut and closely resembled the American GI style. Victoria, meanwhile, gave him a new pair of diamond earrings – David obligingly posed for photographers while wearing them – and the usual furore over his new appearance began.

David was a little bit taken aback by the latest fuss, asking one journalist who kept on about it, 'Do you fancy me or something?' The response was negative, but he was still asked if the style was right for an England captain. 'I don't think it matters,' he said. 'Being England captain is not about the way you look or what you do. Obviously you have to conduct yourself properly on and off the pitch but I don't think it's a problem. It's been made into more of a problem than it should be. Everyone is different. I'm not doing it to create attention. Sir Alex was fine and so, too, was Sven-Göran Eriksson. I don't think he can believe how much is being made of it. He said, if it was your right foot that was the problem, it would be different. Victoria loves it.'

And, at last, David's people sat down to work out a new contract with United. He was in no hurry to get anything resolved, not least because it was still not clear whether Ferguson would be staying on as manager. There was also the added factor that David was now worth a lot of money to United. They could choose to sell him now, if they wished, for an estimated £30 million whereas, if they waited until his old contract expired, he could walk away and they would get nothing. If they wanted to keep him, therefore, it was in their interests to get him signed up.

David was asked if he wanted to know what the situation was before deciding anything. 'Yes,' David replied, 'and as I've said already there is no rush to sign a new contract. It would be interesting to know who is coming in but I don't think the board or anyone else is going to tell me. I have two years left [on the old contract] and I will have to wait and see what goes on and what is said in the talks. The talks only started 11 or 12 days ago and I don't expect them to be completed this summer. I'm not going anywhere, though. As far as I am concerned, I will be reporting back to United at the start of the next season and the manager will be in charge. If the club did want to sell me, that would hurt. I love Manchester United. I have been here for 10 years and I have been a supporter of the club all my life. You can never say never about playing abroad, but right now United is where I want to be.'

An added complication for United was that the club now had more people to deal with: Tony Stephens, David's long-term agent, and members of the Outside Organisation who represented Victoria and, at her instigation now had David on their books, too. Again, it led to some concern over the influence Victoria was having over her husband's career – but, as long as David wanted it that way, there was not a great deal anyone could do.

And he continued to model for magazines. His latest appearance was on the cover of *The Face*, in which he appeared to be spattered with blood (it was actually soy sauce). He then suffered a real injury – a groin strain in a match against Aston Villa – after which it was feared that he would not be able to play in the crucial World Cup qualifier against Germany in Munich. This put David in such a black mood that he couldn't even speak to his father during a two-and-a-half-hour car journey, while Victoria had to endure a week of gloom. In the event, he was able to play, but felt he'd behaved so badly to everyone that he even apologised publicly. 'I was really down after the game, I couldn't speak to anyone,' he said. 'I don't think Victoria has seen me in this sort of mood before. I'm in a mood when we lose but I'm terrible when I'm injured. I'm saying sorry to her now. It has been difficult.'

To everyone's utter delight, England beat Germany

5–1, an outstanding result and England's biggest ever win over Germany. David didn't score any of the goals – Michael Owen, in a game he'll always remember, scored three – but played beautifully, again justifying Eriksson's decision to keep him on as captain.

'It was one of the proudest moments of my life,' said Victoria, who had clearly forgiven him for grumbling. She had watched the match from Leicester, where she was performing. 'David was brilliant. He led from the front like a general and I'm not ashamed to admit I was in tears. He was under so much pressure to deliver the result England wanted. But typically he came off the pitch and congratulated everyone else. He has given the country something to shout about. They are all heroes out there.'

David was, indeed, in typically generous form. 'Everyone showed great character after we went a goal down so early on,' he said. 'We just tried to get the ball to Michael Owen and Stevie Gerrard as much as we could.'

And Sven? He was absolutely delighted – and as coolly detached as ever. 'We have to forget about this game and concentrate on the one we have on Wednesday,' he said, referring to the forthcoming match against Albania. Clearly, no one and nothing was going to ruffle him – a quality that stood him in good stead when he went on to have ructions in his own personal life.

As the scale of the victory began to sink in, it was

hailed as a victory for England that was second only to the 1966 World Cup. And David had been the captain. When the team went to change after the match, they felt as bemused as everyone else. 'We sat in the dressing room afterwards just looking at each other as if to ask, "What happened there, then?"' David revealed. 'When the world looks at the scoreline, they will be as amazed as we are.' David also said that Eriksson had offered to substitute him before the end because of that groin strain. 'Who would want to miss out on the finish of a night like that?' he asked. 'The moment I will remember most is walking over to the England fans at the end to celebrate. It was an amazing feeling. As the goals started to go in, we kept looking around at each other like we were all thinking, "What the hell is going on?" You could see it on the faces.'

But although the team were allowed a night of celebrations, the next morning it was back to England and straight back to training. Sven-Göran Eriksson might have been ice to Sir Alex Ferguson's fire, but both had exactly the same attitude when it came to keeping their teams ready and fit. After the training session, however Eriksson did allow his men, who were staying in Slaley Hall Hotel in Northumberland, some time off. Some played golf – the others went shopping.

Of course, when everyone calmed down, they realised there was still some way to go. Germany was still top of the qualifying group, with England three points behind, which meant the forthcoming matches against Albania and Greece were crucial. David was well aware of this. 'The whole nation was behind us in Germany and will be behind us in Newcastle,' he said. 'There'll be no problem about lifting the players for the Albania game, but people need to be patient. Remember it took us more than 70 minutes to score in Albania and their defence could again cause us some problems.'

As David and his teammates prepared for their next match, the extraordinary hold the Beckhams had on the affections of the country became yet more apparent with the appearance of something called The David Beckham Effect. *FHM*'s *Bionic* magazine surveyed 3,000 men throughout the UK and found that a massive 88 per cent said that love and affection, rather than beer and one-night stands, were what they wanted most from life. Of the men surveyed, 85 per cent said that sex can stay good in a long-term relationship, two-thirds said their best ever sex was with their wife and 70 per cent said they had never cheated on their girlfriend. It was a long way from laddishness – and it was all down to one D Beckham.

'The family man is cool again,' said Phil Hilton, editor-in-chief of *FHM Bionic*. 'Beckham more than anyone personifies the new dad – not the old dad who bought his clothes from a camping shop and spent his spare time in a shed on the allotment.' It is fair to say that when you start being cited as the cause for national trends, you have made your mark on the country.

David returned to *Parkinson*, this time with

Victoria at his side. On the show Mrs B sang 'IOU', a song she had written for David, to which he responded by wiping away a tear. Her new album, *Not Such An Innocent Girl*, had just been released, and David loyally assured everyone that he loved it. 'It's not my kind of music, but her album has actually made it into my car,' he said. He then informed a startled Parky that he had actually contemplated killing himself when he was falsely accused of cheating on Victoria, before the lady herself lightened the atmosphere by revealing that she calls him 'Goldenballs'. The nickname stuck.

And David proved that he deserved it a week later when England played Greece, resulting in a 2–2 score. The England team as a whole were lacklustre, allowing Greece to build up to 2–1 until David single-handedly (or footedly) saved the day with an injury-time free kick to equalise the score. 'It's the best feeling ever. We didn't play the prettiest of football,' David said after the game. 'We got a goal back and then they got another one and so we had to keep on battling. For a young team to come back from 1–0 to 1–1 to go 2–1 behind and then come back to 2–2 again, it shows the character of the team and how much we all wanted it. It was a good time to score and one that had to go in. I'd had quite a few free kicks and I'd been a bit disappointed with most of them. And then when I got my chance, Teddy Sheringham said, "I'll have it," but I said it was a bit too far out for him and I fancied it.

We kept on battling and we got our just desserts in the end. We wanted to go to the World Cup finals and we are there now.'

Even the normally cool Sven-Göran Eriksson was carried away, racing down on to the pitch to congratulate his team. 'I'm very happy today, of course,' he said. 'It was a marvellous afternoon because we didn't play that well, especially in the first half. The Greeks deserved 1–0 at half-time. The second half we did much better and showed a lot of character. We were a bit unlucky they scored again. It was a marvellous end to a football game. Beckham scored the goal and it was really deserved. It wasn't a winning goal but a drawing goal, which was enough. He played one of the best games I have seen him play. He ran all over the pitch. He was a big captain and if we want to do well in the World Cup, we must do that again. He did everything today to push the team to make us win the game. That was the first step to something that could be very beautiful. Let's be happy today, tomorrow let's try to be better.'

As was becoming usual these days, the whole country cheered Beckham for his performance. England fans danced round Trafalgar Square, singing, 'There's only one David Beckham'. There were tributes from everyone, including, of course, Victoria, who was in Italy. 'I told you David was called Goldenballs – and today he showed the whole world why,' she crowed. 'I am so proud of him and the whole team. I was in tears when I phoned him up after the game. It's going to be so exciting going to the World Cup. I won't see him for a week as I'm on tour in Europe, but I'll be having a drink for him tonight!'

David celebrated by taking his parents, parents-in-law, son, sister-in-law, her daughter and assorted others to dinner at the Indian restaurant Shimla Pinks in Manchester. The chef made a surprise cake for him and the whole restaurant gave him a standing ovation when he blew out the candles. 'I think David was genuinely surprised by the reception he got,' said the restaurant's owner, Nisar Khan. 'And he made sure he thanked the other customers by asking us to hand a piece of cake to everyone. That is the type of person he is. He wanted everyone to enjoy the moment and share in the celebration.'

It was hardly surprising that the jubilant David went on to say that he wanted to play in every game he could. Sir Alex wanted to rest him during United's forthcoming match against Olympiakos, but David persuaded him otherwise. 'I don't want a rest, particularly when things are going so well,' he said. However, Fergie did manage to get Beckham to take a weekend off, which he spent jetting to see Victoria, who was now in Scandinavia. And who can blame him for such overexcitement? To go from villain to national treasure – there were even calls for him to be knighted – would please anyone and David, a modest and emotional man, found it especially overwhelming.

He also made peace with Germany by appearing on a chat show with Victoria. For the occasion he wore a £20,000 watch, a £15,000 ring and £5,000 earrings – even more jewellery than Victoria was wearing. 'I'm just a regular bloke,' insisted David, before winning the hearts and minds of the audience when he was asked about German coach Rudi Voller. 'He's an excellent professional, a great guy and a great footballer.' That one was greeted with wild applause. David looked ready to conquer the world.

Chapter Thirteen

There's Only
One David Beckham

As Christmas approached, Manchester United had still not come to an agreement with David over his contract. This was becoming a real problem. Christmas had been set as an informal deadline for the talks and, if a deal were not sorted out by then, there was a real possibility that United would sell David the following summer, when he had a year left to run. For a start, there was disagreement about the money involved and, on top of that, SFX favoured a mere two-year extension. United sources claimed that they were near to fixing terms but, interestingly, David had actually started asking colleagues about life abroad. It seems that, as far back as the end of 2001, he was beginning to realise where his future might lie.

But he was still England captain and as such he had responsibilities to pursue – sartorial ones. Much to the amusement of onlookers, Sven-Göran Eriksson had asked him to dress the England side for the World Cup, prompting much ribaldry about sarongs. David responded with dignity. 'It's my job as England captain to organise things like the suits and pick the colour and style of them,' he announced. 'Normally the manager has a say but Mr Eriksson said, "Let him do it." They won't be anything like the Liverpool cream suit or anything flash either. They will be very normal.'

Given David's status as national treasure, it was almost inevitable that he would be named BBC Sports Personality of the Year for 2001 – and he was. More than 750,000 people had voted: Beckham, dressed as a Chicago gangster, dutifully thanked his family, Sir Alex, Eriksson and, of course, Victoria and Brooklyn. It was a generous gesture. David had again been dropped from the United line-up against West Ham – and United had lost. There had been some muttering that, had David been included, the outcome would have been different, but no one was in the mood to spark yet another public row. In fact, David went on to say that Fergie had been right to drop him.

The very next day, David won another award: Britain's Best-Dressed Man, beating the likes of Robbie Williams and Jude Law in a poll of *Heat* magazine readers. Shortly after that, he was runner-up for the

FIFA World Player of the Year awards for the second time in three years, losing narrowly to Real player Luis Figo. But still the rumblings of discontent went on. Despite his public statement, David was said to be increasingly angry that Ferguson kept dropping him. United, meanwhile, claimed that David had a bad back – and there was speculation that the real cause of the problem was the amount of money David was demanding. David was sanguine. He went shopping.

Christmas passed with no resolution to the problems, which promptly resurfaced in January. Sir Alex put David on the starting line for the first time in seven weeks in a match against Fulham, but Beckham was not at his best, and was dropped again in the next match with Newcastle. He kept publicly stating that he wanted to stay at United, but observers were beginning to ask, if he was never going to play, what was the point? Sven-Göran Eriksson wasn't happy, either. He would not have dreamed of criticising Sir Alex publicly, but an England player needs to play and David was not getting much chance to do so at the moment.

And the problem with the contract had still not been resolved. United were aware that, if they didn't tie David down by January 2003, he would be free to sign a pre-contract agreement with another club, but the various advisers simply could not agree. There was not only the money to think about, there were also lucrative image rights. 'Both sides are frustrated,' said

Peter Kenyon. 'You do reach a point where you can't go further and after several months of good negotiations you also reach a point where you conclude things one way or the other.' The other, of course, referred to selling David.

David played on. Victoria, meanwhile, admitted that actually she had had some influence on her husband's fashion sense and particularly disliked the way he wore his trousers high up his body. 'It was a case of, "Those trousers, what size are they, sir? Aren't they irritating your nipples?"' she said. 'Me and Britney [Spears] can both pick men that aren't really that great [Britney was at the time dating Justin Timberlake], change the clothes, change the hair and they're pin-ups.' It was not the timeliest of interventions. The last thing that David needed at this stage in the game was yet more speculation that it was actually Victoria who was in charge.

There was at least one step forward in February 2002 when, after months of speculation, Sir Alex Ferguson confirmed that he would be staying on as manager. 'I am over the moon. We had been hearing the rumours about the manager not retiring, but we didn't believe them,' said David. 'But he came in before training on Tuesday and told us.' It emerged that Sir Alex's wife Cathy had persuaded her husband to stay on. 'We all know about wives always making the decisions!' chirped David. He also revealed that negotiations were finally moving forward with his own contract. A salary of £70,000 a week had been agreed and now the two teams had just to sort out image rights.

It was at this point that it was sadly revealed that David's parents were divorcing. Sandra had started the proceedings the previous October, but it was only now that the split became public. His parents had been together for 32 years and David was distraught. He went to pay them a secret visit. 'David is terribly upset because he adores his mum and dad,' said a friend. 'He went to see them this weekend because he wanted the chance to speak to them and see if he could smooth things over to some extent. David is a realist – he knows if the situation has gone as far as the court then there's not much hope of them getting back together. But he is finding it very hard seeing them not getting on with each other so much.' Indeed he was. For a man who was so famously happily married, it was a dreadful wrench to see his parents at war.

In his autobiography he described his parents' marriage and that might have given a clue as to the reason for the split. 'Dad loves my mum,' he wrote. 'But he's never been affectionate to her in front of my two sisters and me and cooks only once in a blue moon. He's quite hard-faced and can be sarcastic. He also gets fired up easily. If something is said about me, he'll want to punch whoever said it. If my mum hears it, she'll just want to cry. The quality I least like in myself is my short temper. I think I got it from my dad.' Clearly David's marriage, full of affectionate gestures all the time and one in which he played an equal role around the household, was very different from that of his parents.

However, nothing – even this personal trauma – could put a stop to the Beckham bandwagon and David's latest £1-million venture was announced at the end of February: he was to design clothes for Marks & Spencer. It was to be a range of boys' clothes and who better than Beckham, with his joint love of football and fashion, to be linked with it? 'David Beckham is the perfect icon for this boyswear range,' said Michele Jobling, the project's managing director. 'Not only is he the number-one sporting hero but he is also a great style icon and role model – we are thrilled to have him on board.'

David was clearly delighted with his new role. 'For some time now,' he said in a statement, 'I have been enjoying the creative side of my commercial work and, when Marks & Spencer offered me the opportunity to actively assist in the design of clothing for youngsters, I was delighted. I want to help create the kind of clothes I would have worn as a youngster.'

It was turning out to be an action-filled year for David. Hardly had the dust settled on the announcement when there was more excitement. Victoria was expecting a second baby and another announcement followed. 'This has been such an exciting year for us – England are in the World Cup finals, Victoria's had a second Top 10 hit and now we are expecting a new baby,' it read. 'It's fantastic. Brooklyn is really looking forward to having a little brother or sister to play with.'

Indeed, both families were delighted. David's father Ted was in Manchester to watch United play Aston Villa and drove Victoria to the game. 'I wouldn't have thought this will be the end of it,' he said as the family prepared for a champagne celebration. 'Victoria has said she would like a lot of children and I know David would, so I'm sure there will be more.'

Sandra might have been estranged from him but she agreed. 'We're all really thrilled about the baby and I can't wait for it to be born,' she said.

There were similarly supportive remarks from the Adams family. The dynasty was set to continue.

And it was celebrated in a slightly unusual fashion. Sikh twins Amrit and Rabindra Singh painted a picture of the family, representing them as Hindu gods. David, complete with four arms, was Shiva; Victoria, wearing a cocktail dress and holding a microphone, was the mountain goddess Parvati; and little Brooklyn was their son Ganesh. The painting went on display in Manchester, with the twins explaining, 'They are figures people follow just like gods in the Hindu religion. It is not blasphemous.'

An image of David also appeared in Madame Tussaud's in a new attraction called Goal! He had finally caught up with Victoria, who had made it to the waxwork museum three years earlier.

The announcement of the pregnancy also meant that David was keener than ever to stay at United, as this was not the time to cause upheaval. 'United is the only environment I've known,' he said. 'I have so many friends around me it's difficult to imagine how I might react to anything else. I'm talking about real friends here, not just workmates.'

Sir Alex was equally eager to finalise contract details and David continued to pay tribute to him. 'Of course, I respect him because, for a start, he's the reason I'm here,' he said. 'And that goes for a lot of the other players here as well. I think we all realise that, without Alex Ferguson, we might not have progressed in the way we have. He's the one who gave us a chance and had faith in us. He believed he had some youngsters who could come all the way through. I think our respect for him stems from that. In spite of what anyone says, there's never been a problem on that score.'

The couple celebrated Brooklyn's third birthday in typically lavish style: they threw a £3,000 bash at Manchester's Printworks Complex and laid on a private screening of *Monsters Inc*, followed by clowns, conjurors and a huge birthday cake iced in the colours of Manchester United. As before, the party was attended by a number of David's teammates and their children, while the birthday boy and his father had double cause for celebration. David was voted Britain's Best-Dressed Man in a poll by *GQ* magazine – while Brooklyn also made the list at number 17.

David and Victoria were in party mode. They followed Brooklyn's celebrations with the announcement of a World Cup party, themed 'White Tie and Diamonds', to be held in May at Beckingham Palace. And contract negotiations were at long last complete: David was to receive a £70,000-a-week salary, with a further £20,000 a week for his image rights. It was a relief for everyone. David was now tied to the club for the foreseeable future – on top of which he was now one of England's best-paid footballers.

As the World Cup approached, all eyes centred on David's every move on the pitch. There were serious fears that he might have been badly injured when he was tackled by Diego Tristan during a match against Deportivo La Coruna and had to be stretchered off the pitch. This came right after Sven-Göran Eriksson warned, 'Injuries are the only big worry that I have. If I go to games and see a player on the ground I just cross my fingers.' David's injuries, however, proved less serious than originally thought, with Ferguson commenting, 'He could be back next week.'

It was a relief all round. David had matured so much, both as a person and a player, that playing without him would have been a serious blow. 'I think it would have been a big problem if he was not fit to lead England in this summer's finals,' said England legend Sir Tom Finney. 'He is one of the biggest influences on the rest of the side. He doesn't get involved in silly things like he used to.'

World Cup star Ray Wilkins agreed. 'We would really have suffered without him,' he said. 'He has proved over the last few games that he is a real lucky talisman for England.'

As David recovered from his injury, he could at least console himself with the fact that he was now the richest sports star under the age of 30, overtaking the previous year's incumbent, the boxer Naseem Hamad. Together, he and Victoria were now estimated to be worth £35 million, according to the *Sunday Times* Rich List, where they came in at 962 out of the top 1,000. And he needed the good news. A week later, back playing against Coruna, he was again stretchered off with a broken foot. Beckham was in tears on the touchline before being taken off to hospital in an ambulance, accompanied by Victoria. Ferguson said he would be out for 'six to eight weeks' and was doubtful whether he would be fit enough to play in the World Cup.

After taking medical advice, it was decided that, with intensive treatment followed by a special training programme, David would be able to play, but would miss out on the remaining United games of the season. 'I do not need to find a new captain for the World Cup,' said Sven-Göran Eriksson. 'I have one already – his name is David Beckham.'

Ferguson was also more positive. 'He has a good chance of going to the World Cup,' he said. 'At this moment I'd say it's very doubtful he'll wear a United shirt again this season.'

It was ironic. At the end of the previous year, when David had wanted to play, he had been confined to the bench. Now, when Ferguson was playing him, he was stuck in a hospital bed. David himself was rueful. 'Having seen the newspapers in the last few days, the media focus seems to have been mainly around the World Cup, whereas I have been thinking about the Manchester United games I have been missing,' he said sadly. 'The season has been building up to a great finish and I wanted to play my part in another triumphant year. The messages of goodwill I have been receiving have been overwhelming – I have always said that Manchester United fans are the best in the world and times like this remind you of just how great they are. I will be joining them in the stands for the next few weeks, giving the lads every support as they try to make another great year for everyone connected with the club.'

Poor David. It was a very unfortunate accident, and a painful one at that. 'The foot was a bit sore going into the game, but that was just fluid on the foot after being tackled in the first leg the week before,' he said. 'I knew it was a bad tackle as I went into it. I felt the pain but, because we had a free kick, I jumped up to take it. But I felt it a bit and the referee made me go off the pitch. I limped off and took my boot off. I told our physio Rob Swyre to spray something on it, or put some water on it. But, as soon as he'd done that, I put my foot on the floor and felt it crack. That's when I knew it was broken. Victoria is five months pregnant, but she's the one who is running around and getting me cups of tea!'

As usual with David, his injury made the front pages – and as for it being his left foot that was broken, one supporter wrote to a newspaper saying, 'I didn't know he'd got one.' An oxygen tent was installed in the Cheshire apartment to aid David's recovery and David was given ultrasound therapy. Meanwhile, well-wishers were even leaving get-well cards around David's waxwork at Madame Tussaud's. The Prime Minister sent a good-luck message. The world, as usual, went mad.

David was not so caught up in his own problems, though, that he could not think about other people's. On the ITV programme *Tonight With Trevor McDonald* David revealed how the brave terminally ill six-year-old Kirsty Howard had moved him. Kirsty was born with a back-to-front heart and nine other cardiac abnormalities and was raising money for her hospice: so far she had raised £1,250,000 out of a hoped-for £5 million. The previous October the England team had adopted her as their mascot and a month later David and Victoria attended the hospice's annual fundraiser, the Angel Ball. 'I didn't think anyone would mean as much to me as Kirsty would until I actually met her,' he revealed. 'She is such a courageous little girl. All I can say is she touched me, she really touched me. I'm quite an emotional person, anyway, and I've certainly become more emotional since meeting Kirsty.'

Kirsty herself was thrilled to bits with her new friend. 'He came to my Angel Ball with Posh – and I didn't know,' she said. 'When they walked in everyone clapped and we had our photos taken. Then he kissed me again – that was so brilliant. I had a white dress on and a halo with tinsel. He said I looked like an angel. They came and sat with me and Mum and Dad at our table, and I sat on his lap. Posh said that I am allowed to hold his hand – but she says that she won't let any other ladies do it. That's special, isn't it?'

Kirsty was also concerned about David's broken foot. 'I've had lots of kisses off David now,' she confided. 'But I kissed him first – then he scored a goal for me and it made him happy. He makes me happy, too. When I sent him a get-well card for his foot, I wrote lots of kisses inside. I did seven because he wears the number seven on his shirt. I said, "I hope your poorly foot gets better soon." He had to go to hospital and he's got crutches. He can't run after Brooklyn, either. I've played with him and Posh gave me a Barbie doll Brooklyn got for Christmas. But if Becks takes his medicine and keeps his leg up in the air, it might be better quick and he can score another goal in the World Cup – like he did for me.' It was a typically generous gesture from David – and one that Kirsty's parents appreciated enormously.

David had now become so popular that he chalked up another first: appearing on the cover of *Marie Claire*. In its 14 years of UK existence, the magazine had only ever featured women on the cover, but was prepared to break with tradition for its June 2002 issue because it was Mr Beckham. 'When it came to putting a man on *Marie Claire*'s cover for the first time, there was only one candidate – David Beckham,' said the magazine's editor, Marie O'Riordan. 'He represents something for every woman – father, husband, footballer, icon. In a word he's the ultimate hero.'

David was also pretty pleased. 'That's what made me want to do it, because I'm the first man ever to go on the cover. I was like, "Wow!"' he said. 'I was so excited about doing the shoot.'

As ever, David came across as the consummate new man in the interview, kicking off by talking about how much he fancied Posh pregnant. 'I think it is one of the sexiest times in a woman's life when the little bump starts to appear,' he said. 'I find her really attractive when she is pregnant.' And what of the rumour that David is an animal in bed? 'That's definitely one of the true ones!' David replied.

David went on to talk about how flattered he was to be fancied by men, adding, 'I'm very comfortable with it.' This was just as well, since he was interviewed at around the same time for *GQ* magazine by David Furnish, Sir Elton John's partner. 'When I looked at Victoria for the first time I felt real love,' he said. 'People will probably go 'Ugh' and find it sickening when they hear that. As soon as I saw Victoria, that was it. When I saw the video of her wearing a catsuit in the desert, I was just, "Phwoarh."'

No one was saying 'Ugh' – rather, they were falling over themselves at how adorable David was. Could it get any better? Yes, it could. In mid-May the couple held their 'White Tie and Diamonds' party, which was an enormous success. The £350,000 bash was held in an enormous marquee in the Oriental garden at Buckingham Palace and had a Japanese theme: geisha girls greeted the guests, who included Sir Elton and David F, Joan Collins and Percy Gibson, Sven-Göran Eriksson and Nancy Dell'Olio, and Jamie Oliver. Also present were Emma Bunton, Cilla Black, George Best, Mick Hucknall, Natalie Imbruglia and others too numerous to mention – including swarms of footballers, a busload of Buddhist monks and Mohammed Al Fayed, who arrived in the Harrods helicopter.

No expense had been spared for the party, the proceeds of which were to go to the NSPCC. The marquee – which covered over half an acre – was hung with lanterns and candles, and decorated with 60,000 orchids. Sushi was served, along with beef satay, monkfish, bok choi cod and stir fry. Inside, the party was split into four zones: a Japanese water garden, a nightclub, a forest and a dining area. Entertainment was provided by Beverley Knight, with Radio 1's Dreem Teem taking over in the evening.

David and Victoria themselves looked spectacular: David was wearing a knee-length button-up black jacket with sides slashed to the waist, matching trousers and sandals, designed by William Hunt. To adorn it he wore a deep red silk sash around his waist and diamond earrings. Victoria, meanwhile, was sporting a black £15,000 Ricci Burns dress. It was an off-the-shoulders design, which showed off her pregnancy-enhanced cleavage, slashed to the waist and topped off with a leather coat. The couple could not possibly have looked more radiant or more glamorous than they did that night.

'If you thought the wedding was camp, you haven't seen nothing yet,' said a jubilant Victoria. 'This is camper! David and I don't throw parties very often but when we do, we like to do it properly. At the end of the day, it is for a very serious cause, but we have to have a bit of tongue wedged into our cheek. All I have got to do is hold my shape together until the end of the party, then I can just let it all hang out. I've bought the Rolls-Royce of paddling pools. I'm just going to wallow in this thing all summer. No one is going to see me and I'm just going to swim about – it's going to be fabulous.'

Victoria was talking on a programme to mark the occasion in support of the NSPCC. David was also featured going to meet a group of youngsters at an NSPCC centre in Bow, east London. He told the children that he wanted four or five offspring of his own and that he liked rap music – but Victoria wouldn't let him play it in the car when Brooklyn was with them. He also gave them some words of encouragement. 'I have not been through half of what you've been through, but we've got to stay strong,' he told them. 'With me with the World Cup, there was a moment when I had to be strong. It's nice for me to come down here and meet you all.'

Making a speech at the party a couple of days later, David referred to meeting the children. 'Sorry for reading from the cards, it's a pretty daunting experience being up here,' he said. 'I was sat in front of 20 youngsters and every one had an attitude. Everyone was very unsure about me. To see the turnaround in the children within 20 minutes from when I first walked in – they were looking at me very strange – to laughing and joking with me. That was one of the most rewarding things I have done in my career.'

And on that positive note, the team were off to Japan for the World Cup. David had chosen Paul Smith suits for the 23 players and they all looked very smart as they trooped on to a specially chartered plane at Luton. They were also presented with goodie bags, with the contents chosen by David, containing £4,000 worth of designer luggage, state-of-the-art laptops and CD players from Sony, and silver Paul Smith cufflinks. The first stop was Dubai, where the team were to spend a few days resting with their wives and children in attendance, before going on to the Far East.

Victoria, who had been planning on staying behind, changed her mind at the last minute and decided to accompany her husband. There were still some anxieties about David's state of health, to say nothing of the fact that he had put on half a stone. David sought to allay the nation's fears. 'It is just a question of regaining my fitness now, and that's not a problem,' he said. 'I put on a little bit of weight, but it won't be a problem getting it off. There are ways of getting my fitness back other than playing in the pre-tournament games against South Korea and Cameroon.

'If I went into a tackle in one of those games, I could end up doing the same thing again to my foot. I have to be careful with it because if I do come back early there is a chance it will crack again. That's why I am taking my time. I probably could kick a ball in a week but I will leave it as long as I can. Kicking a ball won't be a problem but the first time I will take any risk with the foot is in the first game against Sweden. That's the first time I'll risk it in a tackle.'

As befitted England's best football players, the team stayed in Dubai's Jumeirah Beach Club, where junior suites – the hotel only has suites – start at £700 a night. Each came with a personal maid, dining rooms and gardens, bathrobes monogrammed with the guests' initials, swimming pools with music playing underwater – and even outside air conditioning.

The Beckhams stayed in one of the hotel's two aptly named Paradise Suites – Sven and Nancy got the other – for five days before the team itself headed on to Korea and the wives and girlfriends went back home. David and Victoria looked thoroughly miserable to be parted, hugging and kissing at the airport before engulfing Brooklyn in a family hug.

'It was like a scene from an old romantic movie,' said an onlooker. 'They seemed so sad at having to part. David looked really sad. He didn't smile once. Everyone knows he's a family man and it showed. He and Victoria had each other's hands on their knees and were really close. They kept swapping little kisses on the lips and cheek between whispering to each other. David bent down to hug Brooklyn tightly. Then he stood up and hugged Victoria. Both looked close to tears and she was very sniffy. David was really choked. You could see it in his eyes. It was as if the World Cup was miles away and he just wanted to be with his family.'

But the World Cup was just around the corner and Japan couldn't wait to welcome David. He is, if anything, an even bigger star in the Land of the Rising Sun than he is in Britain and David knew that, after the stopover in Korea, he was guaranteed the kind of welcome usually reserved for rock stars and royalty. In Japan there are over 100 websites devoted to him, he makes the covers of magazines on average seven times a week and his autograph is available in Japanese – the only European footballer to have been accorded this honour.

'I do get a lot of attention but I have never experienced anything like it is when I have been in Japan,' said David. 'It is absolutely mad. You only take one step outside your hotel room and you are surrounded by 50 people in the corridor. I tried to go shopping but they had to literally close the entire shopping centre. There were all kinds of people – kids, girls. It is nice, but mad.'

It was also all about to start again. The World Cup 2002 lay just ahead.

Chapter Fourteen

Be-Ka-Mu

Tokyo – indeed, the whole of Japan – was going Beckham-mad. Posters of him were dotted all over Japanese buses, women's magazines featured him more heavily than ever and his number-seven strip was being bought up by thousands of young fans. They called him Be-Ka-Mu, the nearest version of his name in katakana, the system of characters used by the Japanese to describe foreign words.

The Japanese actually prefer baseball to football and so the real reason for his popularity was his appeal as a very handsome family man. 'He appeals to the Japanese because he is good-looking, well behaved and shows that he loves his wife and child,' said Monica Gillett of the British Council, Japan. 'Young people in Japan are looking to Britain and Europe for fashion and ideas. Football is the perfect answer for those who want an alternative to baseball and sumo wrestling.'

To make the point, the British Council actually circulated 200,000 pictures of Beckham on cards to Japanese children, explaining the rules of football and offering useful phrases such as 'Nice move!' and 'Get stuck in!' Crowd violence, incidentally, is almost unheard of at Japanese football matches. The fans sympathise when their team play badly, rather than hanging up effigies outside pubs.

Back in Britain, at the beginning of June, it was the Queen's Golden Jubilee weekend. England was to play Sweden on that Sunday night and Beckham sent out a message to the fans at home. 'I feel proud to be England captain and know that there are so many people back home willing us to do well,' he said. 'Everyone is patriotic about the national team and it has been proved since we qualified. It's a massive weekend. Everyone is going to have a good time and – fingers crossed – everyone will be just that little bit happier on Sunday night.'

He went on to rally his teammates. 'I've got a feeling my time has come – this will be my proudest moment in football,' he said. 'I am a patriot and to be leading out not just any England team but this England team is going to be a special moment for me. There are no nerves. We are young, talented and hungry. We've got an unbelievable spirit in the camp and only winning interests us. We want the World Cup!'

And, of course, David went on to praise Sven and the players. 'The manager helps,' he said. 'You have all seen how laid-back he is and that makes all the players feel at ease. That's good for the players. When you are young, you don't worry about the nerves. I've never been a nervous person on the pitch, you just go out and play. I can handle the pressure. When it is thrown at me, I can kick it straight back. One of Alex Ferguson's sayings is that, if you can turn round to the person next to you and feel lucky that they are there, you'll be OK. And I feel I can do that. I can do that with every one of the players out there. With the talent we have got, we can just go out and play. The expectations are high, but rightly so.'

David's parents had come out to Tokyo to cheer him on. 'This is wonderful,' said Ted. 'Now we can't wait for the real football to begin. All I can say is good luck to England and I hope David plays well.'

Victoria was being as supportive as she could be from the other side of the world, admitting that she phoned David up to 10 times a day. But the match against Sweden turned out to be something of a damp squib, resulting in a 1–1 draw. David was firmly upbeat. 'We're playing one of the best teams in the world, so we've got to believe in ourselves,' he said on the eve of the next match – against Argentina. 'That belief after the game on Sunday was down a bit. We admitted that, but we've lifted ourselves back up now. Our expectations as a team and players are very high. We've set high standards and when they drop we get disappointed.'

Pausing only to buy a kimono for Victoria, David led England out against Argentina. And this time it was personal. Four years ago, Argentina had turned David into a hate figure: now was the time for revenge – and he got it. In the 44th minute of the game, England was awarded a penalty kick, which David took. As he readied himself, the Argentinian did everything to put him off: Pablo Cavallero, the goalkeeper, shouted out where David should aim the ball, while his bête noir, Diego Simeone, shook his head gravely. David completely ignored them – and scored, ultimately leading England to a 1–0 victory.

As David scored, the Sapporo stadium erupted. So did the pubs and bars of Britain: city streets had been visibly empty while the match was on as everyone and his wife gathered to watch the match. David's redemption was complete: he was now officially the greatest living Englishman.

'It feels better than it did four years ago and it's just unbelievable,' a jubilant Beckham said after the match. 'It's been four years since the last time and a long four years. So that tops it all off.' It was difficult, he continued, 'because of the antics of the keeper telling me to put it one way and Simeone coming to shake my hand. But we've done well and worked really hard for this. The team was absolutely brilliant for the whole 92 minutes.'

The team held a party that night to celebrate at their

hotel – although, mindful that there was more to come, no one drank too much and some of the players stuck to fruit juice. But spirits were high, so much so that the team broke into a rousing rendition of 'Don't Cry For Me Argentina'. Meanwhile, the hotel – the Sapporo Kita-Hiroshima Prince Hotel – laid out a huge congratulations banner and decked the reception area with St George's flags. David's parents were in attendance, while back in Britain Victoria was beside herself with joy. David had called her straight after the match and both were so excited, they later confessed, they hadn't known whether to laugh or cry.

The next day it emerged that Victoria had been worried about David taking a penalty in case it further damaged his foot. 'Just before we left to come out here, Victoria actually said, "Please don't take any penalties,"' said David. 'I said to her at that point I would definitely take the penalties. So she knew at one point I would have to but I don't think she realised it would come in the Argentina game. She watched the game with Brooklyn. I spoke to him after the game and the first thing he said to me was, "Good goal, Daddy," so that meant a lot to me.'

It had also been an extremely brave act. As David himself admitted, had he missed, against Argentina of all teams, he might well have been at square one again. But he took the risk – and it paid off.

From that moment, it got better. England went on to draw with Nigeria and then beat Denmark while, to the additional delight of England fans, Argentina crashed out of the World Cup. David's young friend Kirsty Howard sent him a good-luck letter, prompting a return telephone call from David to thank her for bringing him luck. England were now through to the quarter-finals and there seemed a real chance that they would pull through to the very end.

The outcome of the match against Denmark lifted Beckham-mania to even greater heights. More than 5,000 fans besieged the team bus to get a glimpse of David on the way to training, while the hysteria generated by his appearance meant he wasn't allowed out alone. And, unlike the other players, he didn't even have the consolation of his wife flying out to be with him. All the other wives and girlfriends were coming to Japan – Sven had promised the team this treat if they beat Denmark – except David's.

They had been apart a month now, but Victoria was seven months pregnant and it was felt it would be too risky for her to travel. Instead, the couple spoke on video link and on the phone. 'It is important she looks after herself and the baby at this stage,' said David. 'It might be a bit lonely for me, but I would rather Victoria and the baby were safe at home than me worrying about them coming over here. It's past the date when it would be safe to travel.'

It turned out that England would be playing Brazil in the quarter-final that Friday – and it was in that match that the dream was shattered. Brazil won 2–1, leaving the entire team devastated, but especially David. He felt he'd let the country down, despite repeated assurances from everyone, including Victoria, that he'd done exactly the opposite. 'Throughout this competition, I've always had a sneaky feeling that we could go all the way,' he said sadly. 'I told everyone I had this belief we could do it. I thought we had the beating of Brazil, especially in the first half [when England scored a goal]. If we had gone in 1–0 up at half-time, who knows what would have happened? Once they got that goal, it was all a different story. It was a terribly difficult time to concede a goal. Then to leak another one straight after half-time made it even harder. In the end, it just wasn't meant to be.'

On his return to England, David cheered up a little bit. For a start, he was reunited with Victoria and Brooklyn – they had been apart a total of six weeks. And he began to realise that, far from vilifying him, the whole country was proud of its returning son. Meanwhile, his own son greeted him with the words 'I love you so much, Daddy', which did an enormous amount to lift his spirits. Indeed, he felt so much better, he was even able to get Brooklyn's name embroidered in gold on one of the back seats of his new £165,000 Bentley, his 27th birthday present from Victoria.

And, now that Beckham was back, the couple returned to their normal lifestyle with gusto. For a start, they hired some staff – and it wasn't just any old staff. John and Nicky Giles-Larkin, who were taken on to look after Beckingham Palace, had been previously employed by the late Queen Mother and had, in fact, been offered jobs by Prince Edward and his wife Sophie.

'She is delighted to have headhunted royal staff,' said a friend of Victoria. 'She knows the Palace servants are the best in the world and she wants people she can trust.' The couple were to live in a gatehouse on the edge of the Beckham's estate.

Next up, the couple decided to make a fashion statement and, when they attended the star-studded christening of Liz Hurley's son Damian at the Church of the Immaculate Conception in Mayfair, the two sported matching pink nail polish, on top of which David had gone blond. The usual media furore ensued, and even Sir Elton John, a fellow guest and someone more than capable of making a few fashion statements of his own, teased David. Beckham, as usual, took it all in good part.

Clearly planning to stay at United for many years to come, David then bought a £1.25-million barn conversion in Cheshire. With Brooklyn three years old and a new arrival expected shortly, the old flat had just become too small. The new place was just two miles away in Nether Alderley and a spectacular house: it boasted five bedrooms, a gym and a 35-foot pool, as well as half an acre of grounds. It was the perfect place to bring up a family. 'The place is amazing and absolutely ideal for raising kids,' said a neighbour.

Revelling in his new status as national icon, David

then participated in the launch of the Commonwealth Games: he, Sir Steve Redgrave and Kirsty Howard met the Queen at the City of Manchester Stadium and in a glittering ceremony handed her the Jubilee Baton, which held a message from the Queen and began a round-the-world journey from Buckingham Palace in March.

As if all this were not enough, a huge painting of Beckham was then unveiled in the Pantheon, a classical building at the Stourhead, Wiltshire, a National Trust-owned landscaped garden, as part of a month of displays and events to re-create how the gardens looked 200 years ago. The painting, by Barry Novis, showed David in full England kit, arms raised in triumph, and stood among figures including Hercules, Bacchus, Isis and Diana.

'The garden in the 18th century echoed with references to heroes and gods of the ancient world,' said Stourhead's gardener, Richard Higgs, 'a philosophy we have brought to the 21st century by placing a modern-day hero alongside these classical models.' Kathryn Boyd, a spokeswoman for Stourhead, added, 'In the 18th century these figures were a very important part of the symbolism of the arts and the English classical movement. But today we don't relate as much to them, and Beckham was chosen as a more relevant character, a dramatic analogy, a modern hero – and also as a bit of fun.'

In mid-August there was a pregnancy scare as Victoria thought the baby had stopped moving. Two weeks before she was due to give birth, David drove her to Macclesfield District General Hospital, where she was able to listen to its heartbeat.

'When she arrived she looked very worried and stressed,' said an observer. 'She couldn't feel the baby moving in the womb. When she heard the heart beating, she was so relieved she burst into tears. She was very emotional about it. All sorts of worries must run through someone's head when they are pregnant.'

Indeed, everything was fine. Two weeks later, on 1 September 2002, Victoria gave birth by Caesarian section to the couple's second son, a 7lb 4oz baby whom they called Romeo. David was present – having driven down south after playing in Manchester United's 1–1 draw with Sunderland on Wearside the previous day – and emerged from the hospital beaming. 'It's always nervous having children, but it's the most beautiful thing in the world,' he said. 'Romeo's gorgeous. Victoria's great. She's sitting up in bed and the family are here.' And why the unusual name? Because they liked it, David replied. 'Romeo looks like Brooklyn,' he went on. 'He's got Brooklyn's nose and Victoria's chin. I was there when Romeo came out. Brooklyn came in when Romeo came out.' And would David be aiming for a five-a-side team? David laughed. 'Maybe. We might work on that.'

Both sets of parents came to visit, along with Victoria's sister Louise and her husband and children. Ted was unable to contain himself. Contacted later by the press, he said, 'I don't really want to say too much at the moment. I spoke to David. He said, "Don't say anything," but I'm over the moon it's a boy. With my coaching and David's coaching, he should have a good little side there.' Victoria was 'brilliant' he continued. 'She's tired but it's superb. I'll have a drink later on and celebrate.' Asked about the name he said, 'It's David's and Victoria's choice, so obviously it's what they wanted. It is unusual. It's the same as Brooklyn. But I know, if he turns out half as good as Brooklyn, he'll be wonderful. The name's quite catching.'

The nation was perplexed. Not only could no one work out why the name was chosen, but also the whole country had been expecting a girl. There had been reports, a couple of months previously, that Brooklyn had blurted out in a shop, 'I'm going to have a little sister called Paris,' but if he did, he had either misunderstood or he had become as adept at media manipulation as his parents. As for the name, there was one hint that it might have been inspired by David's love of garage music. One particular favourite group was So Solid Crew, especially MC Romeo.

'Big up, Becks,' said the singer himself. 'It's a great name. But then again, I am biased.'

David was unable to stay long: the next day he had to go back up north to resume training. But Victoria's mother was on hand to look after her daughter. Two days after the birth, she and Brooklyn went to the hospital bearing several bags of designer wear for newborns – and a silver football. They had been to Bobbit and Doodles, which specialised in very expensive clothing for children. 'He has been bought some designer babywear, jeans, sweatshirts, teddies and other bits and pieces,' said a source at the shop.

David lost no time in having his Adidas red boots embossed with the name. 'Romeo' was stitched on the tongue just above Brooklyn, just in time for the Premiership match against Middlesbrough, and flown to Manchester from Germany. 'We had a race against time to get them to Old Trafford before kick-off, but we knew what it meant to David,' said an Adidas spokesman.

Three days later, David escorted Victoria from the hospital, using the usual procedure, involving a couple of cars and the back entrance. 'They were fine and seemed very proud of the baby,' said personnel services manager Chris Jones. 'They were all very happy, they went away very happy.'

It was a timely moment to launch the range of Marks & Spencer's children's wear designed by the proud father. The DB07 range, for which David was paid £2 million – he was contracted to produce five collections in all – featured sporty T-shirts, wide-leg tracksuit trousers and zip-up jackets, and he was clearly delighted with his new role. 'When Marks & Spencer offered me the opportunity to actively assist in the design of clothing for youngsters, I was delighted,' he said. 'I want to create the kind of clothes that I would have wanted to wear when I was younger. Having

Brooklyn helped me a lot. I like buying him outfits that I think look good on him and that's the style I wanted to go for with these clothes. The range includes two larger tops I'm sure Victoria will want to wear.'

Towards the end of September, David achieved yet another ambition: to captain United in the Champions League against Bayer Leverkusen. It was only to be a one-off as Roy Keane was only temporarily away and David had often said he knew he'd never get the position while Keane was there, but it was a testament to the faith that Sir Alex had in him and it made subsequent events all the sadder. It also marked David's tenth year with the club.

'I have to admit, I never had David down as a captain,' said Fergie. 'But the thing that impressed me was how well he responded to being made captain of England, because I honestly never saw him as a leader of that nature. He was always a quiet lad in the dressing room with us. But the way he fitted into the role of leading England has been fantastic and he's improved as a player through that. That's why I appointed him captain while Roy is out. David rarely misses a game for us and you don't want to be changing the captain every two or three games because of injury. Back when he started, he was just skin and bones, but you could tell he had a special talent and it was just a question of him filling out.'

But there was an ominous hint of what was to come. 'I think David's best when he's concentrating on his football with us,' Ferguson continued. 'He has a high profile and it's difficult to say how young people handle that. All I can say on the matter is that David's incredible in the way he handles it all.' Sir Alex may have been paying tribute to David's ability to cope with his high profile, but it looked like he didn't like it.

David remained blithely unaware of the matter and promptly made an appearance in the middle of Manchester wearing something that looked like an Alice band in his hair, but which was actually called a Flexicomb. Onlookers actually stopped and stared. 'It's not the sort of hairdo you'd expect to see on a top footballer,' said one. 'I bet he'll get a lot of stick about it in the Manchester United dressing room.'

It wasn't just the Mancunian shoppers who commented on the new style – yet again, it made almost all the papers. As ever, David shrugged it off.

In early October, David was invited to a reception at 10 Downing Street, along with the rest of the England team. Just for once David was not the centre of attention: all eyes were on Nancy Dell'Olio, who had arrived in a striking red outfit. Sven had recently been in the news himself because of a dalliance with Ulrika Jonsson and Nancy was quite pointedly showing the world what Sven saw in her.

In November, Victoria was again at the centre of a security scare when four men and a woman were arrested for conspiracy to snatch her. It was the second time she had been the subject of a kidnap attempt, this time thought to be for a £5-million ransom. It later emerged that the threat was not quite as serious as it first appeared, but at the time David and Victoria were horrified.

'I'm incredibly grateful,' said Victoria after the arrest. 'It's scared the life out of me. I'm stunned by what has happened today. It's terrifying to think that someone would want to do that to you and your children. I'm in absolute and total shock. We have good security. We are very aware of the risks. But, if people want to do this to my family, how can you be 100 per cent sure you'll prevent it? If someone is that mad and that sick, what can you do? I don't think this will sink in for a while. I'm just so shocked.'

David was deeply shocked. 'The first role of a father and husband is to keep his family safe,' he said, before ordering increased security at his home. More CCTV cameras were fitted at the Hertfordshire mansion and more security men and equipment were installed. Sir Alex reacted with kindness, and offered David time off to spend with his family, although in the event David decided to take his mind off his worries by training. Indeed, he felt it would be giving into the would-be attackers if he didn't play.

David's friend Gary Neville vowed support for the player. 'It's not the first time, nor will it be the last, that this type of thing has happened,' he said. 'It's because of who he is. We have rallied around him and supported him. He should not have to deal with the things that he does. It's just the world we live in and it's not right.'

David showed up at training and was deemed ready to play in the Worthington Cup against Leicester – if, that is, Sir Alex picked him. 'David will be considered, but I will make a final decision about that tomorrow,' said Fergie. 'Knowing David, he will want to play – he always does. He likes training and he likes playing football. Obviously, if it was really necessary for him, of course we would have given him time off. But the thing is under control. The police have acted with great alacrity. They have done their job well. There is no threat to David so therefore it is business as usual.'

David did play and ended up slamming home a late penalty, with United winning 2–0. Matters calmed down slightly after that, although the family remained more security-conscious than ever, even ordering a bulletproof car.

Even so, it had been an unpleasant shock and so where better to unwind than a health resort? For once this was not a case of David discovering his feminine side – rather, it was Sven-Göran Eriksson's idea. The whole team was taken to Champney's Health Resort in Hertfordshire for a three-day rest, combining therapy with training. Sven was his usual laid-back self about the whole thing. 'When you're in charge of a national team, you very seldom see your players,' he said. 'It's more difficult to have an atmosphere and spirit like a club where you see them every morning. So hopefully the players will like this break and become closer to each other. I think me being close to the players is good – although, as in life, I don't like just sitting with them chatting about nothing. But, if I have something to tell them, I'll do that.'

David had to miss the first day but bonded happily with the rest of the team on the break. And having met Tony Blair at Number 10, he was now moving in still more exalted circles when he went to Buckingham Palace to see the Queen. A special reception was held for the England football squad and the Football Association, and it emerged that even the monarch had heard about the kidnap scare.

'She raised the subject of security and if anyone's going to know about that, it's the Queen,' said Beckham. 'We spoke about increased security and how it would change our lives. It will definitely change things but it's just something that has to be done. She does know about football but spoke about security. It's something on my mind and obviously something the Queen lives with every day.'

David took Victoria and the boys to Barbados for a much-needed break, but on his return he was appalled to find untrue rumours about his private life were in circulation on the Internet, originating from the website Popbitch. After the trauma of the last month, he had quite clearly had enough and, after announcing there was absolutely no truth in the gossip, contacted his lawyers to threaten legal action. It did the trick. 'There was stuff on the website last week that was untrue and libellous about David,' snapped his spokesperson. 'We sent a legal letter telling them to remove it. They have done that. If anyone repeats it, they will be sued.'

After all the drama of the last months, David needed some light relief and got it by having Romeo's name tattooed on his back, while joking that there was still room for a few more. Going on BBC1's *Breakfast with Frost* alongside Sven-Göran Eriksson, David also tackled the thorny subject of his hair. He styled it himself, he revealed, saying, 'It's whatever I feel like when I wake up in the morning.' And did his mother ever comment? 'She does,' said David. 'She tells me if I look silly at times, but thankfully it's not that often – well, in my eyes, it's not that often.'

And, given security scares and Internet rumours – to say nothing of the furore surrounding Sven's private life – was the price of fame getting too high to pay? 'I think something needs to be done about certain things but, you know, it's part and parcel of being a footballer and being a manager these days,' David replied. 'It's unfortunate that your private life comes into the game because, at the end of the day, all I've wanted to do is to play football all my life. The other thing has to come with it, the fame and everything else, but I'm a footballer. It's hard to come to terms with certain things, but, you know, you can cope with it.' Of course, it helped that Victoria was also so famous. Just as they did in the earliest days of their relationship, the couple relied on each other to help them rise above all the madness.

David's tattooist, Louis Molloy, elaborated on his latest artwork. 'Everybody's seen the angel figure on his back – now I've put wings on it,' he revealed. 'Where the angel's head is bowed, we've put a halo above it. Then we've put Romeo's name above the halo. The whole thing took about two hours and he's very pleased with it. Becks told me he fancied having as many as five kids, so it looks like I'm going to be busy.'

As Christmas approached, the Beckhams had Romeo baptised and prepared to face a gruelling year ahead. Quite how gruelling it was going to be was still not clear. David's profile was set to rise higher still, with him now famous in just about every country in the world outside the States. He and Victoria now could not so much as change their hairstyle without commanding blanket coverage and, given that both were prone to doing just that at the drop of a hat, they were to become more exposed than ever. If anything, the couple seemed to have stepped into the gap left by Princess Diana. They were young, beautiful, vibrant, rich – and, to cap it all, they were in love.

But one person who, despite his kindness over the kidnap scare, was getting increasingly sick of the circus surrounding Beckham was Sir Alex Ferguson. He had seen David grow from a short, shy boy from south London to a global icon, whose fame seemed sometimes to eclipse his football. Worse still, he had become interested in fashion and, worse even than that, he often seemed in thrall to his wife. But worst of all was something Sir Alex really could not tolerate. David was now so famous he was actually bigger than Manchester United. And, in Sir Alex's eyes, no one gets bigger than the club.

Chapter Fifteen

Manchester 2003

At the start of the new year, it seemed nothing could mar David's golden existence. Victoria and the children were at the centre of his life, he was at the peak of his powers as a footballer and he was, to put it bluntly, rolling in it. At £3.5 million a year from United, he was one of the best-paid footballers in the country and his sponsorship deals now included Police sunglasses, Brylcreem, Marks & Spencer, Vodafone, Adidas, Pepsi and Rage Software. He had three houses, each one a mansion, a vast car collection and everything in the world to look forward to. What could possibly go wrong?

Very ironically, David kicked off 2003 by starring in an advertisement for Pepsi that also featured Real Madrid's goalkeeper, Casillas. The two could have had no idea that just six months on they would be playing for the same team – indeed, they were cast opposite each other as the good guy and the villain in the ad, based on the classic *Gunfight at the OK Corral*. It showed David riding into town with four compadres: his United teammates Gary Neville, Juan Sebastian Veran, Ryan Giggs and Ole Gunnar Solskjaer. David walks into the bar, demands a Pepsi – and Casillas drinks it. David orders him outside. The two engage in a penalty shootout. The end.

David certainly looked the part even if he didn't quite sound it – that voice again – prompting speculation that an acting career might be on the cards. And, again, he was being hailed as a thoroughly modern icon for our times. This time round it was a piece of serious academic research: a study called 'One David Beckham: Celebrity, Masculinity and the Soccerati' by Dr Andrew Parker of Warwick University and Professor Ellis Cashmore of Staffordshire University. The work was done for a conference examining the growing phenomenon of sports stars as celebrities and it certainly didn't hold back, claiming that David was the most influential man in England by transforming male attitudes towards love, babies, sex, laddism and homosexuality.

'David Beckham is a hugely important figure in culture and probably now the most influential male figure for anyone in Britain aged five to 60,' said Dr Parker. 'By defying expectations in areas such as what clothes men are allowed to wear, he has helped create a complex new concept of masculinity. That has already begun to change male behaviour and has the potential to encourage a whole generation of men who admire him to act more like him.'

It was heady stuff and there was a good deal more to come. 'He is "new man" (nurturer, compassionate partner, paternally adept) and "new lad/dad lad" (soccer hero, fashionable footballer, conspicuous consumer), while still demonstrating the vestiges of "old industrial man" (loyal, dedicated, stoic, bread-winning),' they wrote. 'Despite his high profile and the ridicule he risks, Beckham stands resolute: bucking the "macho" trend, setting his own agenda, showing support for his wife, playing the perfect father, remaining every mother's favourite – while at the same time, on the field, displaying the spirit and patriotism of a national ambassador.'

Could it get any better? Yes. David was praised for his love of Victoria, fashion and ballet, pretty much in that order, and subverting every male stereotype you can think of. 'He has broken so many strict traditional working-class masculine codes of behaviour that he has the potential to influence lots of boys and young men to do the same – for example, accepting homosexuality as a part of life,' said Dr Parker. 'We hope a spin-off will be to make the world a better, more tolerant place. Although Beckham is still "one of the lads" because he's a footballer, we never see him out drinking with the lads because he prioritises quality time with his family, which is highly unusual in the world of football. In terms of the gender order, Beckham is a law unto himself.'

Was this the straw that finally broke Sir Alex's back? To see David praised for the very qualities that he had grave misgivings about? To hear that David, the young boy he had sent to Preston to get him toughened up, was now the most influential man in Britain?

And, if all that were not enough, David insisted on putting his caring side on display yet again when Wayne Rooney, aged 17, became the youngest England player in history. David, of course, was going to be there for him. 'I used to go to Alan Shearer if I had a problem and Wayne can come to me if he needs any advice,' said the soft-spoken star. 'He's a quiet lad and, if he wants to talk to me, he only need ask. I wouldn't change a single thing from my past, even though I've had many ups and downs. I've stayed balanced through the good times, got through the bad times and became a better person for it.' It wasn't the sort of thing Roy Keane came up with. Is it any wonder Sir Alex felt a pang of downright despair?

Whatever the state of the tough old Glaswegian's feelings, it was less than a week after all this that a football boot flew through the air and connected with David's forehead. From that moment on, there was no going back.

The signs had been there from the very beginning

and for some time now they had been flashing as brightly as the light on top of a police car. When Victoria's autobiography, *Learning To Fly*, had been published in 2001, she described Sir Alex as 'vindictive', said he never said more than 'hello' to her and revealed he 'went berserk' when David asked him for an additional two days off for his honeymoon. However, just as David had always said, she revealed that, despite all this, she'd always encouraged him to stay on at United. When it was finally time to go, the decision was not hers – nor even David's. It was down to Sir Alex.

And so, inexorably, a chain of events that had really started that day in a hotel room, when David first laid eyes on Victoria in the video 'Say You'll Be There', finally came to a head on 10 June 2003 when David learned, in the most brutal possible way, that he was no longer wanted at United. The phrase 'end of an era' is used too often, but this time round it really was the case.

And it was not just David, Victoria and the children who were caught up in the drama. Quite a few Manchester United fans were upset, including one Ted Beckham, David's father. He had been growing apart from his famous son for some time and the news that David really was leaving was a dreadful blow. He gave an extremely frank interview to the *News Of The World* describing his distress. 'I've lost him. That's how I feel,' he said. 'I'm upset with the way things have gone. We've lost that comradeship we had

271

between us. Unfortunately, David has got bigger than anything we could have dreamed of. I haven't told him how I feel. But football was my life, his football was my life and, once you have it, you don't want to lose it. It will be even worse now that he has gone to Madrid. My biggest fear is that it is all over for us. I still have to work and I can't afford to fly over to Madrid every week. When he was at Manchester United I could pop in the car and drive up the road. I can't do that now.'

Ted went on to talk about how David's relationship with Victoria had changed the relationship between father and son. 'He is a bit distant now but he has his own family,' Ted told the paper. 'When you get your own family, you tend to drift away from your mum and dad and that is what David has done. We would talk every day. I am nosey. I always wanted to know what was going on. I am a football fan and I was interested in him. He doesn't speak to me about certain things any more but he is his own man now. I don't see him as much now as I did – I've only seen him a couple of times this year. I still speak to him regularly but we don't see him half as much as we did.'

And one of the reasons, of course, is that David and Victoria spent a lot of time with the Adams family. On top of that, Victoria now wielded a huge influence over her husband. 'People say Victoria controls him and I think it is fair to say he isn't totally in control,' said Ted. 'But I have to be clear, he doesn't do anything he doesn't want to. He's stubborn like me. We [the two sets of parents] have had no bust-ups. Victoria's dad is entitled to his view, that is no problem. I am entitled to mine. David and Victoria do spend more time with Victoria's parents than us. Definitely. I don't think it is anything sinister, it is more of a girl thing. Girls are close to their mums and Victoria is like that. I am not sure we can be part of that as well. We are from different backgrounds and I can't see it. It is difficult. Trying to mix all of us would be impossible. I don't think it is the background thing. If people like me, they like me. If they don't, they don't.' Poor Ted was clearly utterly devastated and he wasn't the only one. David was feeling pretty upset by everything, too.

Still, life must go on and, when the going gets tough, the tough go shopping. David clearly decided that his wardrobe needed sprucing up before he went to meet his new masters and so went on a spending spree at Dolce & Gabbana. It was a spree with a difference. David phoned the shop in advance to let them know he was coming – and then sat outside in his car as staff scurried back and forth between the pavement and the shop.

'I recognised the limo when it pulled up as he has a personalised number plate on it but most people had no idea who was inside the car,' said one astonished onlooker. 'We were all expecting him to park up and stroll into the shop as he has done so many times before.

But, instead, one of the staff inside braved the rain and handed over a suit inside a specially sealed bag. I bet even the Queen doesn't get that kind of service.'

And so it was off to Madrid for that televised medical, after which David was promptly nicknamed 'Golden Bull'. He was then taken off to meet his new teammates and handed his new team strip with his name and number 23 on it by the legendary ex-player Alfredo di Stefano.

'David Beckham is a symbol of our time, a symbol of a post-modern era,' said club resident Florentino Perez. 'David Beckham is a great player, whose dedication and spirit of sacrifice for his comrades has been experienced by all. He is one of the best British footballers of all time and for that reason, and only that reason, is he with us today. We signed him because he is a great football player who dreams of football and who dreamed of playing for this team. David played at the Theatre of Dreams with Manchester United. I would now like to welcome him to the Team of Dreams.'

David was gracious in response. '*Gracias*, Senor di Stefano, Senor Perez, ladies and gentlemen,' he said. 'Of course, I love my family. I have a wonderful life. But football is everything to me and joining Real Madrid is a dream come true. I'd just like to say thank you to everyone for coming and joining me on my arrival, and gracias. Hola Madrid!'

This was greeted with massive cheers from assembled fans. At this point an 11-year-old boy broke free from the stands, dashed across and engaged David in a kick-about before receiving a signed shirt.

David then went on TV to talk about his new club. 'I will try to learn the language as quickly as possible,' he said. 'Brooklyn already knows how to say hello and goodbye in Spanish and I'm sure he'll be bilingual before me.

'It's not my aim to be a big star. I've come to play with all the great players here. That's all. I'm just a footballer. I don't have any problems controlling the fame aspect of my life. It doesn't interfere with the football side, which is the most important. I'm an easy-going guy who does things like going to the supermarket. I'll carry on doing that in Madrid. Doing normal things keeps me grounded, it keeps me balanced.'

Victoria also rose to the occasion, looking stunning in a white suit, hooped earrings and leopard-skin top. She was presented with a white cat from one of the fans who said, 'I just wanted to give her something in the colour of Real Madrid.'

It turned out that it was Victoria who had persuaded David to take the number 23 shirt. It was a very diplomatic move. 'It was difficult to persuade David that 23 was the right shirt number for him, because he told us that seven was the shirt number he really wanted, even though he never thought twice about demanding it from Raul,' said Jorge Valdano. David had originally been offered number four, the shirt of former captain Fernando Hierro, or number 23.

'So we were stuck in the middle of this discussion about whether the number four or the number 23 was the one he should choose and although he pointed out it was a bad idea to postpone the decision, we couldn't reach a conclusion until his wife intervened. She turned to him and said, "Well, Michael Jordan hasn't done too badly with the number 23" and that was the moment we reached a joint decision. I turned to David and said, "23 it is," and that was that.'

Should anyone still be in doubt as to the sheer scale of David's celebrity, the BBC3 show *Celebdaq* released half-year figures about who got the most press coverage. David came out on top, with 200,090 square centimetres of coverage, beating Prince William into second place. Victoria came third, which meant they were the only couple in the top 10.

The couple began planning their move. David had a whole fleet of cars by now and decided that he would take with him his armour-plated Mercedes ML500, his Ferrari 550 Maranello and his Aston Martin DB7. The cost of transporting the cars was £30,000. To be left behind were a Harley Davidson truck, a Bentley Arnage, another Ferrari, a Lincoln Navigator and a four-wheel-drive BMW X5. Victoria also decided to leave her Mercedes behind.

'David's vehicles will really stand out in the club car park,' said a Real Madrid source. 'Most players here are conservative, with BMWs and the odd Mercedes. They are not into supercars.'

An Old Trafford insider agreed. 'Most of the United players are into swish cars, but David was always one step ahead of the others,' he said. 'Most days, the Carrington training ground car park looks like a top-of-the-range dealership, with most vehicles costing more than the average house. Word is that the Real lads aren't in the same league, but they'll be happy to allow him to shine in the car park as long as he shines on the pitch, too.'

In July the Beckham circus moved back to Cheshire, to the wedding of Davinia Taylor, former actress of teen TV series *Hollyoaks*, and sports agent Dave Gardner. David was one of the two best men, the other being Phil Neville. The Beckhams tried very hard not to overshadow the happy couple but it was almost inevitable all eyes would be on them. Victoria looked simply stunning in a peach Dolce & Gabbana gown, while David looked as dashing as ever in a black suit.

And, when you're that famous, absolutely everything you do gets noticed. David was spotted at the fashionable lingerie store Agent Provocateur buying two jewel-encrusted whips and he very nearly splashed out on a pair of furry handcuffs, although he changed his mind at the last minute. The two also posed for Italian *Vogue* and were clearly upping their raunch factor: in one photo Victoria was seen tearing David's shirt off and in another her legs are wrapped around her husband, who is wearing black nail polish and a studded waistband.

With all the fuss, it seemed at least possible that United might have been regretting selling David but, according to Sir Bobby Charlton, life at Old Trafford would go on much as always. 'The fans love this club, but you always get some who doubt us when a big name leaves the club,' he said. 'They always question the decision, like they did in 1995 when Paul Ince and Andrei Kanchelskis left, and when Mark Hughes went. Some people may doubt the manager but he knows what he's doing. Make no mistake. And we back him all the way.'

In fact, to put it bluntly, David was yesterday's news — for United, at least. 'David Beckham has left and that's it,' Sir Bobby went on. 'I like David. He is the England captain and he's a very good player. But my feelings, first and foremost, are for the good of this club. David Beckham is just one player. And he has left us. So, that's the end of it. I've seen many great players leave down the years but we'll go on being judged by our results, like any football club. I'm sure that, if we were to lose our first four or five matches of the season, the critics would love that and everyone would go crazy about us selling David.

'But he isn't our player any longer and we won't concern ourselves about that. We never doubt Alex Ferguson. And, don't forget, you don't make decisions like that lightly and without a lot of thought. Equally, David made a lot of decisions about his future. We weren't the only ones making decisions. People write to me because they think I am the voice of the board. I only reply to the letters that aren't too vitriolic.' Ted Beckham was clearly not the only United fan who was taking David's loss in bad part.

The couple took a quick break in the South of France before resuming their respective careers. In Victoria's case, this meant linking up again with Simon Fuller, the man who made the Spice Girls famous, while David began a tour of Asia with his new club. And the Simon Fuller signing impacted on David, too. Fuller turned the Spice Girls from nonentities into world-famous stars in the mid-1990s and the idea was that he would do the same for the Beckhams. Of course, David and Victoria were already world-famous stars – but not in the all-important United States. And so, Fuller's commission was to turn the family into a brand in itself: one that marketing experts think could be worth up to $1 billion – and that's an awful lot of sports cars.

'The combination of Victoria's glamour and David's sex appeal and sporting prowess could, over the long term, create a $1-billion brand,' said Fuller, now based in Los Angeles with his company 19 Management. 'There are so many great opportunities and exciting times ahead for Victoria and I. Our plans revolve around a mix of fashion, lifestyle, music and television properties. With the Beckham name so renowned the world over, there are no boundaries to what we can achieve together.'

An insider agreed. 'This could be the biggest deal ever,' he said. 'Posh and David are well on their way to becoming the most famous people in the world. Companies will be bending over backwards to be linked to them – they are as famous in the Far East as they are back home. One day the Beckham name could be as famous as Coca-Cola – that's how big this contract is.'

But there was growing acrimony in the background. Ted Beckham was getting steadily more unhappy about the rift with his son – and that rift was growing. David had been very unhappy about his father's outspoken comments about the denouement with Sir Alex and was livid that his father had spoken about the growing estrangement. It finally culminated in a row.

'I don't know if I can repair my relationship with him,' said Ted in an interview in July. 'We've hardly spoken. The last time was when I went over to his house last week. Everybody was there, the whole family and Victoria's family. It was a bit tense. My biggest upset was not being invited to his signing. I'm choked really. I've been there since day one and that really upset me. I'll never forgive him for that. He could have invited me over and said, "I'm signing tomorrow," or whenever it was. That's what upset me more than anything.'

Clearly Ted, like Sir Alex, was not that happy about his son turning into a global icon – but he has. A poll out in July by Virgin Money announced that David

Beckham is the person most of the public would like to see on their banknotes – beating even Princess Diana, and that is saying something. When you have beaten Princess Diana in a popularity contest, then you are truly a hero to the rest of the world.

And so the circus that is life chez Beckham is set to continue and grow ever bigger. For all their many detractors, the pair have clearly touched a nerve with the public: leading extraordinarily privileged lives and blessed beauty, youth and talent, the two look set to continue to soar. David is at the height of his powers and should stay there for some years, while Victoria has actually become genuinely beautiful over the last few years. And their relationship, upon which all the brouhaha is built, is real.

Real Madrid's gain is United's loss. The future is bright. The future is Beckham.